On Golden Pond...
Or Up the Creek?

Making the Right Choices for
Your Retirement Security

F. Bill Billimoria, MBA, CPA/PFS, CFP®

On Golden Pond...Or Up the Creek? Making the Right Choices for Your Retirement Security
Published by Synergy Books
PO Box 80107
Austin, Texas 78758

For more information about our books, please write to us, call 512.478.2028, or visit our website at www.synergybooks.net.

ISBN-13: 978-1-933538-78-5
ISBN-10: 1-933538-78-3

Copyright© 2007 by F. Bill Billimoria

Library of Congress Cataloging-in-Publication Data

Billimoria, F. Bill, 1943-
  On golden pond-- or up the creek? : making the right choices for your retirement security / F. Bill Billimoria.
    p. cm.
  ISBN 978-1-933538-78-5 (hardcover : alk. paper)
  1. Retirement--Planning. I. Title.
HQ1062.B54 2007
332.024'014--dc22

                                        2006102833

In Grateful Appreciation…

Thanks to my wife Helen, and sons Jim and Eric who have put up with me and my work schedule throughout my professional life and, especially, during the time it took to write this book.

Special thanks to my friend and mentor Len Walter without whose encouragement and support my career, and this book, would not have been possible.

Thanks also to my colleagues and friends, Angelo Alleca and Mark Morrow for their unwavering support in trying to get this book published. And to Colleen Coster for her help with the exhibits included in this book.

And, above all, sincere appreciation to all my clients and friends for their faith and confidence in me throughout my professional life spanning almost a quarter of a century.

Contents

Chapter 1

Introduction

YEARS AGO, I SAW the movie, *On Golden Pond* with Henry Fonda and Katharine Hepburn. I remember the idyllic retired life they led; free from cares, they passed the time by fishing and enjoying their grandchildren. They were living the picture that most of us would like to paint for ourselves.

Unfortunately, if we keep doing what we've always done to prepare ourselves for retirement, most of us aren't going to get to live on, or come anywhere close to living on Golden Pond. In fact, to use another familiar term, most of us will be "Up the Creek" instead, and without a paddle, I might add.

Having been in the financial advisory business for more than twenty-three years, I've heard many statistics about the painfully grim financial picture that soon-to-be-retirees face. It is a generally accepted fact within the personal finance industry that roughly 23 percent of people who reach the age of sixty-five (prospective retirees) will have to keep on working. Another 73 percent will be dependent on their family, friends, charity, and even the government to help them make ends meet. In other words, a mere 4 percent of all adults turning sixty-five are financially independent and secure! (I use sixty-five as the retirement age as a default. You can substitute any age at which you want to be "on golden pond"). And with the stock market bubble burst destroying so many nest eggs in 2000-2002, that depressingly low number is dipping even lower, even in spite of the real estate boom over the past several years. Couple that with the fact that life expectancies are on the rise, and it becomes

1

painfully obvious that some prospective retirees have had to push back their retirements. Some may, in fact, have to face the depressing thought of having to work forever! And even if they were already retired, quite a few retirees have had to go back to work to make ends meet. This is not just disheartening, it's appalling.

Considering the technological advances we're surrounded by, you'd think we'd all have a handle on our retirement plans. Look on any bookstore shelf and you'll see a vast array of retirement and financial investment books. Go to the Internet and you will find even more information on personal finance. But despite the fact that these books are record-setting best-sellers and that information on the Internet is so readily accessible, the ratio of people acquiring this information versus actually improving their long-term lives hardly registers on the scale. The information to help and guide you is all out there, just waiting for you to use it. Yet the media keeps telling us that the percentage of financially-independent people over age sixty-five is declining.

Warning: This book takes a sharp right-hand turn away from its predecessors.

I'm not interested in preaching to you. Nor am I going to offer you a dictionary version of every possible financial option under the planet. However, it is crucial that I first help you understand the **Eight Great Barriers to Golden Pond (Chapter 2)**, which are preventing almost 96 percent of our sixty-five-year-old population from reaching their Golden Pond. If you're not sixty-five, I can assure you: **if you don't watch out, these barriers will get you too**. Once you develop an understanding of these barriers to Golden Pond, you'll be able to circumvent, leap over, or bypass any and all of them. I'm going to show you how.

In Chapter 3, I focus on where you are now and where you **want** to be financially. Thanks to medical breakthroughs and ongoing technology, life expectancy is increasing with each passing year. **If you want to retire at sixty-five, you're easily looking at another thirty years of life.**

I know it's hard to imagine, so just take a moment to think back on the **first** thirty years of your life. It may have moved like a speeding train, but it carried with it thousands of days of experience, discovery, life, and love. You have that entire span of life still waiting around the sixty-five-year-old corner! But unlike the first thirty years of life, you don't have the time to make wrong decisions any more. Risky business, financial recklessness, and heart-pounding chances may have been acceptable when you were a young adult, but do you really want to go through all that again? Trust me. You just don't have the time.

I am reminded of a response by a seventy-year-old client of mine after I suggested a long-term investment for him: "Son, I don't even buy green bananas anymore!" Believe me, if you don't have the time for green bananas to ripen, you do not have the time to recover from major losses.

At my seminars, many people (usually in their forties and early fifties) tell me that they want to live out their retirement years at the same or better quality of life that they currently enjoy. Yet they have no idea what this would really cost or what specific measures need to be taken to create this lump sum. Just how much money does it take to live out your thirty-year retired lifestyle without depending on a never-ending job, the government, family, or friends? While this can be a pretty hefty sum, I don't want you to panic. When you panic, you make financially devastating decisions; or worse, you make no decisions at all. If you plan ahead and do it right, it could take a lot less money than you think. This is where we begin to explore your current situation with an eye on reaching that magical place called Golden Pond.

In Chapter 4 I'll be addressing your cash flow and its priorities. What do you **need** to spend, and why do so many other expenses in life take priority over what you **really need** to prioritize? How can you get a better handle on managing your money?

Chapter 5 tackles the two largest destroyers of your financial well-being: inflation and income taxes. In most cases, taxes alone can swipe more than one-third of your gross earnings. Inflation can destroy the purchasing power of your dollar, and the effects of inflation are so subtle that you might not even know that your money is losing its purchasing power until it's too late. There are few things more inevitable than income taxes, but rather than risk the consequences of just *not* paying your taxes (unhealthy tax evasion), consider the solutions that will allow you to keep more for yourself (healthy, safer tax avoidance)! **What's the difference between tax evasion and tax avoidance? About twenty years!** In this chapter, I'll be offering solutions to help you keep ahead of the evil twins: inflation and income taxes.

I call Chapter 6 "Risk Management" because it sounds much friendlier than its real name: insurance. Sadly, the word "insurance" is misrepresented as a rather dull, "have to" expense. And deservedly or undeservedly, insurance agents have the reputation for being "snake-oil" salesmen. All their well-intentioned suggestions are usually looked upon suspiciously by people who could actually benefit from them. Instead, these suggestions are often looked at as ways to make the agent rich at the purchaser's expense. As a result, many people ignore insurance's essential role in the financial picture.

That's sad because insurance really does play a critical role in one's overall financial plan. By ignoring this aspect of their financial life, people often "cut off their nose to spite their face" and jeopardize their chances of reaching the promised land of retirement security. Life, disability, medical, auto, home, liability, and long-term care insurance are all a part of "risk management" and they all have to be addressed to reduce or eliminate your vulnerabilities.

Chapter 7 focuses on investments. Investments are much more than just stocks. In fact, investments can be defined as ways of making your money work for you, be it in stocks and bonds or real estate, even while you try to work for your money. No matter what the skeptics say, **proper investing is the main engine that determines not only your ability to reach Golden Pond, but also the likelihood that you stay there for the rest of your life.** In fact, this chapter is so important and so full of information that I seriously considered creating a complete book on just this aspect of personal finance. If your investments don't perform well, you'll have "engine trouble" at every mile along the way and will invariably stall out before reaching your destination. Throughout this chapter,

I'll explore your alternatives based on your own individual idea of Golden Pond. I'll tell you where investors make their greatest mistakes and how to avoid them.

In Chapter 8, I'll teach you about the "three-legged retirement stool." For decades now, retirees have depended on the three legs of the retirement stool. These legs consist of: 1.) company retirement programs, 2.) government programs (e.g. Social Security and Medicare), and 3.) an individual's own savings.

More and more, the main support for the stool is going to have to be your own individual savings. As the years go by, the role of the other two legs is considerably diminishing. In this chapter, you'll learn how this three-legged stool is being altered and what you can do to personally remedy the situation.

Chapter 9, Estate Planning, focuses entirely on ensuring that your money ends up in the right hands and in the right place after your time on Golden Pond is up. We will discuss ways to minimize the impact of estate taxes so that your beneficiaries and the people you love get most, if not all, of the money you worked so hard for.

Finally, in Chapter 10, you'll learn how to find the right financial advisor. First, I will discuss whether you really need one. If we determine that answer is "yes," you will learn how to go about finding one. I will address questions such as, *What do you ask for? What do you watch for? What kind of advisor best suits your needs? What fees can one expect to pay?* I'll also provide suggestions on how you can make your relationship with your advisor more meaningful and rewarding.

Stop Gambling. Do It Right Once and for All.

At one of my recent seminars on retirement, a gentleman asked me for advice about his retirement, which was coming up in two years. He was in his early sixties, and he had almost no savings, and not much in his IRA or his 401(k) plan at work. He was wondering what he should do. When I found out that his salary was in the six figures and had been for more than ten years, I was astounded.

I asked him what he had done with his money and he replied, "About 90 percent was spent on wine, women, and song; and the rest was spent foolishly." He thought this was a great joke, and I admit that I found it funny too.

However, what wasn't so funny was the fact that this man had invested all of his hard-earned money in the dot-coms in the late 1990's. He had increased his portfolio dramatically the first three years, but had stayed at the party too long His portfolio had lost almost 90% of its value from 2000 to 2002. He was almost without any savings. He had frittered money away, thinking "things will work out eventually." Now, instead of sitting in an Adirondack chair in front of his Golden Pond, he was truly "Up the Creek." There was no way this man was going to have a retirement, let alone a financially-secure one. It was a little too late for him.

I don't want it to be too late for you. If I can help you avoid just one or two mistakes I've seen people make, this book will have achieved its purpose.

Before you start with the next chapter, I would like to remind you that you will come across a lot of exhibits (graphics and forms) at the end of some chapters. If you would like to download or print out these exhibits, please visit the website:

www.GoldenPondRetirement.com

In addition to the exhibits, this website also contains financial calculators, market data, and information about ordering bulk quantities of this book. If you are interested in contacting the author for speaking engagements for your business, trade association, or group on all matters pertaining to personal finance, you can contact him by e-mail at:

Bill@GoldenPondRetirement.com

So let's get out that paddle, shall we? It's time to negotiate our way out of these choppy waters to the smooth-as-glass Golden Pond reality we desire.

Chapter 2

The Eight Great Barriers to Golden Pond

IN A SMALL *town in the Midwest there had been heavy rains and a lot of flooding. Finally, when his house was surrounded by six feet of water, a man climbed up to his rooftop and prayed for rescue.*

Shortly thereafter, two men paddled by in a canoe.

"Hey buddy!" one yelled out. "Get on board; we've got room."

The man replied, "No, thanks. Don't worry. The good Lord will take care of me." So, the canoe went on.

The water continued to rise and began lapping against the eaves of the roof. At about that time, a large motorboat swung by and the driver shouted out to the man to get on board. Again he refused, saying, "No, thanks. Don't worry, the good Lord will take care of me."

Finally, the water was lapping at his neck. At this point, a helicopter showed up with a rope ladder swinging down. "Come on up!" the copilot said, "We're here to save you!"

"No thanks. Don't worry, the good Lord will take care of me."

The man eventually drowned. He showed up at the pearly gates thoroughly irate. "St. Peter," he complained. "I'm a devout believer in God. I prayed for Him to save me. How could you guys let me drown like that?"

St. Peter looks confused, refers to his notes, and says, "I can't understand…according to my records, I sent out a canoe, a motor boat, and a helicopter."

So many times a week I hear people complaining about their financial losses because someone, or something, or even "luck," didn't come to their rescue. Let's forget about luck, shall we? We cannot count on it. Fortunately, aside from luck, there is an abundance of help out there to guide us safely to Golden Pond: books, magazines, newspapers, community colleges, and yes, even the Internet. A good beginning is the book you are holding in your hand right now.

Okay, maybe there is just **too much** out there to the point that you are so confused that you cannot act on your own. In fact, this could very well be a barrier. However, as far as I'm concerned, this is a cop-out, and I don't buy it.

If you are overwhelmed by all of the information out there, you can certainly seek the assistance of a professional advisor who could act as your coach, confidante, and captain of your boat as you make your way toward the security of a comfortable retirement. But **you** are the one who has to take hold of the rope. If you're not any more proactive and committed than the man standing on his roof and expecting the good Lord to take care of him, then you've got no right to be indignant when you find yourself "up the creek" at retirement–assuming, of course, that you can retire.

In a manner of speaking, this book could very well be the first boat for some of you. For some others, it may even act as the second one. And I know, for at least a few of you, this book is going to be the helicopter!

Here's your first step toward rescue:

You've got to know what the Eight Great Barriers to Golden Pond actually are. Even though every case is different, there are common threads that, left unheeded or unnoticed, can destroy your financial security to the point where you find yourself totally up the creek at a time when you do not have much time or wherewithal to turn the boat around.

By getting to know these Eight Great Barriers to Golden Pond and understanding how they could adversely impact your finances, you will be that much better-prepared to start taking control of your financial destiny. This doesn't mean that these eight barriers are the only factors you need to ensure your retirement security. It merely implies that **you will significantly improve the odds of reaching Golden Pond if you familiarize yourself with these Eight Great Barriers**.

Even as you begin navigating your own financial waters (on your own or with a "guide" who thoroughly knows and understands the course you wish to take), you must continue to scan the area around you, and especially in front of you, to make sure that you don't get blind-sided by developments that could easily turn your pond into a dry creek.

OK, so let's get started identifying these Eight Great Barriers. After all, knowledge is power. Pay attention to these eight culprits, and you'll find yourself reaching your goals faster, eliminating many false starts that have the potential to toss you into the rocks.

While I haven't necessarily listed these in order of importance, I'll note that this first Great Barrier is *the* primary reason behind so many failures:

1. Lack of a Plan

"If you don't know where you are going, any road will get you there!"

You **have** to know where you want to go. Do you ever get into your car not knowing where you are going, what road you are going to take to get there, or approximately how long it will take to get there? Of course you don't! Yet, that's exactly how we approach our retirement. We don't know when, where, or how we are going to retire; we just have a vague idea of where we want to be with nothing specific in mind.

In fact, most adults approach their retirement years like Christopher Columbus. When he started out, Columbus didn't know where he was going, when he got there, he didn't know where he was, and when he got back, he couldn't tell anyone where he'd been!

Doesn't that sound exactly like most people's approach to retirement? You bet it does. A cliché in the business states: "no one plans to fail, but most fail to plan!" It is so true!

No matter how smart or educated they may be, most adults don't know what to do or how to go about doing it (and for the record, the statement "I want to be rich" does not constitute a plan). So first and foremost, you've got to establish specificity of objective and time. Before we go very far into this book, I want you to take a long, hard look at your goals and objectives and be able to say: "I would like to retire at age ____ with _____ dollars of monthly income to meet my projected expenses in terms of today's dollars."

"Today's dollars" means that inflation is not taken into account (it should be and will be taken into account later, but for now, the specific objective listed above should do fine). Anything other than a statement showing a specific goal with a specific time frame is nothing more than a pipedream. **It's merely wishful thinking**.

Now, how do you come up with your specific retirement figure? We'll be addressing this very question in the next two chapters, but briefly, it's a matter of evaluating your current expenses against your current income and then looking at what you see yourself doing in retirement.

Where are you now? What are your assets and liabilities? How much longer into the future will you have a mortgage? Will you be increasing your travel or food allowance at retirement? You can bet that medical insurance and medical costs are going to continue to climb. So, how much would you allocate for medical costs at that time? Will you be able to live on 60 percent of what you're spending now? 80 percent? 120 percent? Would you prefer that your lifestyle stay exactly as it is now, or do you want to have more financial freedom in retirement?

Whatever the case, you've got some thinking to do! And a good first step is to figure out what sources of income will be increased, reduced, or eliminated. Ditto for expenses.

Your time frame is equally important. At what age do you want to retire? To some people, the word retirement sounds much too final. They would rather refer to it as "the age they achieve financial independence." By financial independence, I mean the ability to say to your boss, "I quit!" if and when you feel like it. Some people may want to use stronger language, and that's okay.

That's what being truly financially independent is all about, and that's okay too. A piece of advice for you, though: **make sure that your brain is engaged before you put your mouth in motion with your boss.** Make sure you have enough money in your bank account to back up your statement. Keep in mind that you and/ or your spouse could conceivably live to ninety-five or even one hundred years of age.

Now, I am all for early retirement, but the earlier you retire, the longer your retirement nest egg is going to have to last. Retirement at age sixty means you will need enough resources to last until Social Security kicks in at sixty-five or perhaps even sixty-seven, assuming, of course, that it is even around in its current form by that time. Even after your Social Security checks start, do you have the resources to survive another forty years? That's 480 months! Let's say you need $3,000 a month in today's dollars at retirement. That's $1.44 million, not taking into account inflation. Yes, Social Security might offset a part of that sum (a **very** small part!), but the rest will have to come from your 401(k), IRA, and other savings. So, once again I offer a friendly word of advice that bears repeating: before you go around putting your mouth in motion about wanting to quit, make darn sure your brain is in gear. The process we go through in this book should help you to keep your brain in gear.

2. Ignorance

In my seminars, I sometimes ask the attendees if they would consider working for me for one month on a salary of one cent on the first day of work, two cents on the second day, four cents on the third day, and doubling every day thereafter for thirty days. You would be amazed by how many people tell me to "go to Hell!" or "go find another sucker!" The fact is that under that payment plan, my new employee would have to be paid $5,368,709 on the 30th day. And, if the month had 31 days, the salary would be twice that: $10,737,418! Hypothetically, these people turned down millions of dollars probably because they just did not understand math. With a little more knowledge, they would have made the correct decision.

Ignorance is not to be confused with stupidity. Ignorance hinders you from making the right decisions, as in the above example. An ignorant person can make himself knowledgeable and eventually "get it." Stupidity implies a lack of common sense. A stupid person is essentially clueless, and it is highly unlikely that a stupid person will ever catch on. You have to make an attempt to learn at least the basics of personal finance. No, I am not asking you to become a rocket scientist, but some rudimentary aspects of finance are well worth learning. It really is not complicated, and it can even be fun. Remember, it's your retirement we're talking about. If you don't make the effort to ensure your financial security, just who do you think is going to do it for you? **If you don't take an interest in your own finances, believe me, you're asking for trouble**. You will be fair game for every con artist trying to make a fast buck, and you won't even know enough to realize it when you have been had.

This warning also applies to people who try to offload the whole responsibility of their financial picture and planning to a "professional." Trust me, this doesn't work either. You could end up setting unrealistic goals and expectations, or worse, you could trust the wrong person, making yourself an easy target for every fast-talking financial product or strategy salesman who comes along. But even more important than the worry of a "professional" taking all your money and funding their *own* Golden Pond is the fact that no one can build the picture that's in your head. You have to take an interest in what exactly you want to build for *you*. No one can do it for you.

Time is money. Create leverage for your time and your money by increasing your financial knowledge first.

I'm also not asking you to become a financial whiz. I'm merely suggesting that you get to know the basics of finance, like "the Rule of 72," which calculates the number of years it takes to double your money at a given interest rate, or conversely, what rate your money has to earn to double in a certain number of years (**Exhibit 2-1**). It's also important to know the difference between simple and compound interest (**Exhibit 2-2**), the time value of money (also called discounted cash flow; **Exhibit 2-3**), and the definition of a marginal tax bracket versus average tax rate (**Exhibit 2-4**).

These are all facts that you can pick up by going to your local library or even logging onto the Internet. If you are terrified by math, don't worry. In today's high-tech society, financial calculators and computers can do that job for you. **But you have to understand what those numbers mean.** An average person should be able to comprehend financial concepts simply by devoting just one hour a day for no more than one month. Having these basics under your belt will put you miles ahead of the pack.

Please do not tell me that you just do not have the time to learn all of this complicated financial "mumbo-jumbo." It is just a matter of setting priorities. You have to make the time to understand the basics. It's as simple as that. It is a well-known fact in the financial planning community that **most people spend more time in one year planning for their two-week annual vacation than they do in their entire lifetime planning for a thirty to forty-year retirement.** Is it any wonder, then, that only one out of twenty-five people (4 percent) who reach age sixty-five in this great country are financially independent? Yes, you can hire an advisor to do most of the work for you; but it is so much better when you can understand what the advisor has done, why he has done it, and how it affects your future.

At the very least, you should get familiar with the use of compound interest tables. Just do a search on the Internet for "compound interest tables" and you will get several sites that show you how to use the tables in your everyday life. Examples of these uses are listed in the next paragraph. Please note that the terms "interest rate," "inflation rate," and "rate of return" can be used interchangeably in the examples below:

What is the value today (present value) of a sum of money given to me some time in the future at a specific interest rate? We all know that a dollar in the future is worth less than what it is worth today. This table allows you to calculate how much less it really is. This is what economists mean, for example, when they say that a

1968 dollar is worth only thirty cents today thanks to inflation. What is the value today of a sum of money given every period for a specific number of months (or days or years) at a specific interest rate? We all know, for example, that lottery winners get paid a fixed amount every year for a specific number of years. Well, if you won the lottery, by using these tables, you would be able to figure out the true value of the prize you won. And, let me tell you, it is nowhere close to the millions of dollars they claim to be giving away (hey, I am not suggesting you buy lottery tickets to reach your Golden Pond. This is just an example to get your attention!). What is the future value of an amount of money several years from now at a specific interest rate? This is the opposite of what was mentioned at the beginning of this paragraph. How much would the money I currently have grow to at some time in the future at a specific rate of return? What will be the future value of a fixed sum of money deposited every month (or days or years) for a specific number of months at a particular interest rate? This can help you figure out how much you would wind up with at age sixty-five if you decided to invest, say, $100 per month for thirty years (assuming you are thirty-five today) in an investment that gives you a specific rate of return. What periodic deposit will grow to a specific amount at the end of a certain amount of time, at a specific interest rate? If you wanted to retire at age sixty-five with $1 million, this table will allow you to determine how much money you need to save monthly or annually at a specified rate of return.

What periodic payment can be provided by an amount of money today for a specific amount of time at a specific rate of return? If I have a sum of money and I want to get a monthly payout from it for a certain number of years, this table would allow me to calculate the payment I could expect for my retirement, assuming a certain rate of return.

Okay, I can feel your eyes glazing over with the examples I mentioned above, but you have to admit, these tables are extremely versatile. They will help you understand your mortgage loans, auto loans, investments, and even some ordinary day-to-day situations involving money. If you can learn how to use these Discounted

Cash Flow tables (**Exhibit 2-3A**), you are well on your way to becoming a financially-astute consumer. Take the time to educate yourself. It will be well worth it. As the saying goes, "If it's got to be, it's up to me!"

3. Too much debt

If I had to vote on any one barrier that prevents people from reaching their Golden Pond, this has got to be it. This is the one that gets most people up the creek and we see this every day, everywhere. If you are not careful, this barrier will get you, too.

Some immigrants call this country "the land of opportunity," where milk and honey flow through the streets. I call this "the land of conspicuous consumption," where instant gratification and living beyond your means is the name of the game.

Yes, it is true that the American consumer has kept the economy going during an economic slowdown that lasted more than three years (2000–2002). In fact, if it were not for the consumer, we would probably have experienced a major recession during those years.

However, even in good times, the American consumer has always believed in overspending. During and after the most recent economic slowdown, he stepped it up big time thanks to low interest rates. One slight problem: **he has been doing it with money he doesn't really have.**

He has maxed out his credit cards. He has refinanced his mortgage, and then refinanced again, and again. He has bought the latest electronic gadgets, he has bought real estate, he has taken expensive vacations, and he has bought cars. He has spent himself into a tizzy buying things he really doesn't need, all in a never-ending quest to "keep up with Joneses," and all with money he really doesn't have.

The median income today is approximately $44,000 for a family of four, and the median household credit card debt is $8,000. That's almost 20% of your annual pay before taxes! Add to that the fact that mortgage payments and rent account for another 30–35 percent of your gross salary, and you can see the problem we are going to experience down the road.

If you were to pay off the credit card debt, you would have less than half of your income left to pay taxes, buy food and clothing, pay utilities, save for your children's college education, save for your daughter's wedding, for your own retirement, and to replace your car every so many years. So, where is the savings going to come from?

There is no doubt about it. If you find yourself struggling because there is just "too much month left at the end of the money," look to reducing your debt load. **There can be no Golden Pond until this barrier is overcome**. It's up to you to put a stop to it.

Once, a young couple visited me in my office for some financial advice. I was shocked to find that at age thirty, their net worth was a **negative** *$75,000. In other words, they owed more than they owned by that staggering amount. But that wasn't all of it. I had seen them drive up in a brand new Corvette—so new that it did not even have license plates yet. And the car was not listed on their statement of assets and liabilities ("balance sheet," in financial lingo). When I asked them about it, they admitted that the husband had received an unexpected bonus, and they decided to buy the Corvette. It had been purchased after the balance sheet had been prepared, and that is why they had not listed it. They had financed the car with a loan of $35,000! It never even occurred to them to pay down some of their debt with the bonus. Instead they justified the purchase by asking themselves, "Why should we have to wait 'til we are sixty-five years old before we can enjoy life?"*

Well, I am not a betting person, but I could have bet the house that with a debt of $110,000 at age thirty, they would never make it to Golden Pond; at least not until they changed their spending habits dramatically. Unfortunately, there was not much of a chance of that happening because in their minds, they were not doing anything wrong and they really did not have a problem.

The first step in the solution to any of life's problems is to recognize that you have a problem. These people were blissfully unaware of what lay in store for them. What's more, they didn't want to know.

Again, the solution lies in first looking at your income and expenses, your assets, and your liabilities, and knowing what you **can** spend versus what you **should** spend. It means not making a purchase until you have the money to do so. It means whittling down the number of credit cards you own (at last count, the average American owned eight credit cards!). It means using your credit card only as a convenience and having the money in your checking or savings account to back up the purchase. This implies that you pay off your credit card bills for the full amount and not just the "minimum required monthly payment." Believe me, the interest charges on some of the credit card bills are exorbitant and totally unconscionable, but they have been disclosed to the holder of the card, and he is responsible for it. In fact, the interest income is so lucrative for these credit card companies that they prefer for you to take your own sweet time to pay off the bill because then they get to collect on those fat interest rate charges. Credit card companies love to send you unsolicited cards, hoping you will use them. That's how you wind up with twelve credit cards! Do yourself a favor; tear up those cards and those solicitations right now. **Credit is like a drug habit. Once you're hooked, it's almost impossible to extricate yourself from it**. An individual should have one card that is used more as a convenience than anything else. In exceptional situations, you may need two or even three. But twelve? No way, Jose!

The definition of a credit card: "A means for buying something you don't need at a price you can't afford with funds you don't have." It also means looking at and revising your total borrowing picture. Long-term borrowing should be reserved for investing only (e.g. your home or condo), not for spending on day-to-day needs.

If I had to sum up in five words the secret to financial security, it would be **"spend less than you make!"** Unfortunately, most people ignore this simple advice and at retirement, when it's really too late, they find themselves "up the creek!"

4. Bad Investments

Who hasn't invested his hard-earned dollars on a hot tip provided by a well-meaning friend, brother-in-law, or even a stockbroker? Most of the time, these hot tips get you burned. Not only is it illegal to act on inside information (just ask Martha Stewart!), it is usually useless. Unless you really know someone way up there in the company hierarchy, almost all of the "inside information" given to you by a self-professed "expert" has already been factored into the price of the stock. It's too late to act on the information; the markets are just too efficient in that regard. Now repeat after me: "**There is no free lunch on Wall Street.**" In fact, if you do not do proper due diligence, Wall Street will have *you* for lunch.

Too often, people don't want to spend time doing research on their own. Instead, they take the easy way out by following the crowd or acting on the basis of somebody else's research, experience, and bias. **Next to too much debt, this is one of the biggest barriers to Golden Pond**. Investors who bought into the dot-com euphoria, only to crash and burn, have learned to their dismay that their Golden Pond may not only be delayed, but perhaps out of reach forever. Thanks to their greed, these are people who are truly "up the creek."

Remember, "hot tips," "great leads," and "can't-miss opportunities" are phrases that ruthless hucksters use to separate you from your money. We have all heard our parents warn us that "if it's too good to be true, it usually is!" Nowhere is this more relevant than in the area of investing. Investor Beware!

However, the stock market is not the only place where you can make bad investments that set back your retirement. An over-priced real estate deal or an ill-conceived and poorly thought-out business venture can just as easily cause the same catastrophic results. **No matter what the investment, do your homework**. If you cannot do the homework, hire a professional to do the homework for you, but make sure you do your homework on the professional. The fact is, you just cannot escape getting involved. It is *your* retirement and you better take full responsibility for it. Your ability to reach Golden Pond depends on it!

5. Lack of Protection

You can have the most fantastic plans and be well on your way to living happily ever after, but your fairy tale will be shattered if you don't protect yourself against lawsuits, sudden disability, or even death. I will now address the most hated profession in the financial arena: insurance. In fact, the insurance industry realizes this and prefers to call it "risk management."

The importance of insurance can only be appreciated when it's too late.

I know you don't want to talk about it. Maybe you don't even want to think about it. Maybe you don't like insurance people. Maybe the information is confusing, and it's difficult to compare one proposal against another. But **don't be caught without protection.** What happens if one or both breadwinners in the family were to get disabled? Or die prematurely? Or get sued? Or lose their job? A proper risk management program should address all of these vulnerabilities. You don't necessarily need to like the program, but you just cannot afford to ignore it. What's the sense of having an elaborate plan and working hard to achieve your objectives, only to have it all taken away in an instant by any of these potential occurrences?

This aversion to insurance (oops, I mean "risk management") is truly incredible considering the invaluable role it plays in one's ability to reach Golden Pond. In fact, when I am on an airplane and do not wish to be disturbed by the person sitting next to me, all I have to do is tell him that I am an insurance salesman. There will be blessed silence for the duration of the trip. However, the reverse is usually the case if I tell him that I am an investment advisor. In that case, the person next to me will ask me for hot tips, confide in me about his family, his finances, and sometimes even his sex life! He will keep talking endlessly until we finally (sometimes thankfully) reach our destination. Perhaps the insurance industry is to blame for the negative image. In the twenty-three years I have been in the profession, the industry has done nothing to improve the image and credibility.

It doesn't matter if you like them or dislike them. Don't "cut off your nose to spite your face." Make sure you are adequately protected against all the curves that life can throw at you. You and your family will be glad you took care of your vulnerabilities before it is too late. Just like a loan, the best time to apply for insurance is when you don't need it. So, get going and eliminate (or at least reduce) those vulnerabilities… even if it means talking to an insurance agent. The assets you save could be your own. The lives you protect could be your loved ones'.

6. Inflation

I call inflation "the silent bandit" because it can rob you of your purchasing power and you won't even realize it until it's too late. During President Jimmy Carter's term, annual inflation was at an astounding 12 percent! Using "the Rule of 72," that means that expenses were doubling every six years (72/12 = 6). In other words, the purchasing power of your dollar was being cut in half every six years.

If you put a frog in a pot of boiling water, the frog will jump out right away. However, if you put the frog in a pot of cold water and gradually turn up the heat, the frog will boil to death before it realizes what is happening. The effect of inflation is similar to this scenario. That is why it is referred to as the "silent bandit." If you are not watching out for it, your finances, too, could "boil to death" before you realize what is happening to your money.

Since the Carter years, inflation has been tamed to the point where it stands at around 3 percent currently. However, to paraphrase Mark Twain, the news of its death is highly exaggerated, especially for retirees who face sky-rocketing medical care and gasoline costs and, thanks to the recent real estate boom, property taxes that are spiraling upward along with the cost of food. Think it cannot happen to you? Take a look at the inflation statistics shown in **Exhibit 2-5** and see if you still feel the same way afterwards.

Because inflation is such a silent phenomenon, there's a tendency to put off thinking about it. Also, thanks to global competition over the past several years, inflation has been relatively tame. Businesses just can't afford to raise their prices like they once did because they're afraid to lose their market share. They try to compete by reducing costs, laying off employees, cutting expenses, etc.

Because of high unemployment and a less vibrant economy, the federal government lowered interest rates and pumped a great deal of "new money" into the system to keep up consumer spending. While this is great in the short term, it eventually creates too many dollars chasing too few goods (remember, there's less production on the manufacturer's side to cut down on the costs).

What happens as a result? Inflation *has* to creep in. It's inevitable. In planning for retirement, we usually assume an inflation rate of 4 percent unless the client would like to use a higher or lower number based on their own unique situation. At the rate of 4 percent, inflation will cause the retiree's expenses to double every eighteen years (there we go with that Rule of 72 again! See how we use it in finance so often?). So a sixty-five-year-old retiree could conceivably see his expenses double by the age of eighty-three. If he is on a "fixed income," how is he going to meet his expenses at that time and beyond? It behooves every person seeking Golden Pond to take inflation into account. **Ignoring inflation can, and will be hazardous to your wealth.**

7. Income Taxes

It's been said that taxes are the 600-pound gorilla sitting on your ribcage. Unlike its insidious partner, Inflation, the Tax gorilla is a well-known, noticeable entity in our lives. Between federal income taxes, state income taxes, local income taxes, Social Security withholding, and Medicare withholding, the average wage earner could easily wind up losing a third of his paycheck. Depending on income and which city and state a person lives in, the paycheck could easily be cut by a half!

The gorilla has also gotten far more complicated. In 1913, a one-page IRS tax return told you to write down your gross income and then send in 1 percent. More than ninety years later, a new, simplified tax return might as well be made up of just two lines:

1. How much money did you make last year? _____
2. Send it in!

Funny, right? But we are gradually getting to that point.

Then, of course, there is the issue of complexity. Every so often, a newspaper or magazine will run a contest based on a hypothetical case study. The object of the contest is to determine which professional can do the income tax return most accurately. Our tax code is currently such an abomination that in almost every contest, no two professionals have come up with the same answer. Moreover, on several occasions, not a single professional has even been correct!

Regardless of the arcane nature of our tax laws, just keep in mind that you have to allow for income taxes in all your planning. Take a look at Exhibit 2-6 and you will see just how much impact taxes can have on your income. For example, if you are currently making $60,000 per year, your net disposable income could be $45,000 by the time you are done paying taxes. To plan for your retirement based on the full $60,000 being available to you would be foolish and dangerous.

It has been said that only two things in life are inevitable: death and taxes. So, if taxes are inevitable, we must accept the fact that they will never be eliminated. You can, however, try to reduce the tax bite by planning and strategizing. Every dollar you save on taxes that you do not have to pay is a dollar that's going to fund your trip to Golden Pond.

You need to understand the differences between taxable income, tax-free income, and tax-deferred income. For example you can bunch your tax deductions in particular years to meet the minimum limits (2 percent of adjusted gross income for miscellaneous deductions or 7.5 percent for medical expenses) that need to be itemized.

As with everything we have been talking about, if you find taxes too difficult to understand, hire a professional who can help you reduce the onerous burden of taxation. It could not only turn out to be a good return on your investment (they might be able to save you more taxes than the fees they charge!), but it could also help you avoid getting in trouble with the Infernal (I mean, Internal) Revenue Service.

8. Procrastination

I thought of listing this barrier first, but I put it off because I did not want to think about it. *Just kidding!* Jokes aside, this is one of the main reasons why some people do not make it to Golden Pond. **They never get started!**

It's just so much easier to not do something, don't you think? There's always tomorrow, right? And, we're all just so busy with our lives. In our twenties, the last thing we want to think about is retirement. We're too busy figuring out where our next job will be, and who'll be our next date. In our thirties, we are in an "establishment role," whether that be buying property, settling into a career, getting married, or having children. In our forties, we're focused on getting those kids through college. In our fifties, *they're* getting married and, lo and behold, our sixties show up and we've just begun to wonder what we're going to do about our retirement! I hear every excuse in the book for procrastination. Behind every excuse is what I consider a plausible fear that people need to overcome.

It's OK to have the fear, but it's not OK to let that fear rule your life.

As an example, some people are afraid of failure, some are afraid they do not know enough to do it, and some may feel they cannot afford the fees of a professional advisor. Others may be afraid of getting ripped off by an advisor or losing control of their situation. However, the biggest reason people do not act is because they want everything to be just right before they take that first critical step.

Let me ask you something that I often ask the attendees at my seminars: If you drive to work every day, what would happen if you decided that you weren't going to start your car until all the lights between your house and your office were green? You wouldn't even get out of the garage, would you? Yet, this is exactly what we do with our financial life. We wait for everything to be perfect before we do anything. Reality Check! **There will NEVER, EVER be a time in your life when everything is perfect**. Most people instinctively know this, but use that alibi anyway to get away from the fear of acting on something.

You're still not convinced, right? To you, procrastination can't be all that bad. Well, I have proof for you. Take a look at **Exhibits 2-7** and **2-8**. These are two examples that demonstrate just how much the true cost of "waiting" is. Still not convinced, eh? Well, refer to **Exhibit 2-9,** which shows what is involved in trying to accumulate a million dollars by age sixty-five. According to the exhibit, if you start today with nothing and you're twenty-five years old, you would need to invest $2,055 every year at an annual at a rate of return of 10 percent. However, if you're thirty-five years old, you will need to invest $5,527 every year. At forty-five, the amount jumps to $12,392 but the rate of return would need to increase to 12 percent annually. And, boy, if you're fifty-five and are starting with nothing, you will need to invest $50,879 every year with a rate of return of 12 percent. Now you know why people say "Time is money." It truly is.

Procrastination not only costs you valuable time, but consequently, you have to do more to be able to achieve the same in a shorter amount of time. We're normally too slow to react. We don't take fast action; we want to sit and think about it awhile (in other words, we're quite possibly back to the fear of making a wrong decision).

Motivational Speaker Les Brown said at one of his seminars, "You can sit by the pool and read all the books you want on swimming. But you will never be able to swim until you jump in with both feet and swallow half the water!" Folks, the time to jump into the pool is **NOW!** Not tomorrow, not next week, not next month, not next year. It's **NOW!** Time is running out!

In the chapters ahead, you are going to embark upon a journey to get yourself on Golden Pond. Being aware of these Eight Great Barriers will go a long way toward ensuring that you don't find yourself "up the creek" just when it's the time in your life to relax and enjoy the fruits of your labor. It will be a frustrating journey at times. You will even feel like giving up in disgust and decide to take your chances with whatever life has to offer you (we call that "seat-of-the-pants planning"). However, once you see yourself making headway, you will be so fired up that you will want to move ahead and do whatever it takes to make sure you reach that magical place—your very own Golden Pond. You will begin to feel empowered and ready to take on whatever challenges life throws at you. You will feel in control, and rightfully so. After all, you are the captain of the boat that's headed for Golden Pond! I will be there to serve as your guide and mentor and to keep you headed in the right direction. Now let's get started.

Exhibit 2-1
The Rule of 72

The Rule of 72 allows you to calculate the number of years (N) it would take to double your money, given a particular interest rate or rate of return (R) on your investment. Conversely, it also allows you to determine the rate of return that you would need on your investment in a given number of years.

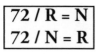

$$72 / R = N$$
$$72 / N = R$$

Similarly, there is also a **Rule of 115** that would allow you to perform similar calculations to **triple** your money.

The table below shows a summary of the calculations:					
Rate of Return	**1%**	**3%**	**6%**	**9%**	**12%**
Number of years to double	72	24	12	8	6
Number of years to triple	115	38.3	19.2	12.8	9.6

Note: These calculations are also handy for determining the effects of inflation. Just substitute the rate of return for the rate of inflation and you will be able to determine how long before the price doubles. For example, at an annual rate of inflation of 9 percent, the annual cost of college education would double every 8 years and triple every 12.8 years.

Exhibit 2-2
The Difference between Simple Interest & Compound Interest

Simple Interest basically implies that you keep earning the same amount of interest every year on your original investment. It does not take into account the interest you would earn on the interest you had already earned. **Compound Interest** does take into account the interest on the interest earned—essentially compounding your interest.

For example, let us say you started with $1,000 and, in twenty-four years, the amount has grown to $16,000. The Simple Interest for the above investment is calculated as:

$$(16,000 - 1,000) / 1,000 = 1,500\%$$

$$1,500\% / 24 \text{ years} = 62.5\% \text{ per year}$$

In other words, you made 62.5 percent per year, or $625 every year on that investment, but did not earn any interest on the reinvestment of the $625 every year. This is not only incorrect, but it could also be very misleading.

However, by **the Rule of 72**, we see that the investment has doubled every six years. Therefore, the **Compound Interest** (Rate of Return) is only 12 percent by the formula in Exhibit 2-1.

Note: It pays to know the difference between these two types of interest because some investment companies try to make their performance better than it really is by using Simple Interest in their advertisements, rather than Compound Interest. You could wind up making the wrong decision based on intentionally misleading information.

Exhibit 2-3
Discounted Cash Flow

Discounted Cash Flow takes into account the time value of money. It is based upon the fact that a dollar today is worth more than a dollar some time in the future, and, conversely, a dollar in the future is worth less than a dollar today. The actual difference in present and future value is based on the purchasing power of the dollar and is affected by the rate of inflation and the level of interest rates.

The "time value of money" calculations help you when you are making fixed payments for several years into the future. For example, your mortgage payments of, say, $1,000 per month today will be the same 20 twenty years from now (assuming you still have the mortgage), but the purchasing power of the dollar would have dropped substantially by then. In other words, you would be using cheaper dollars in the future. The same would apply to your annual life insurance premiums. The borrower is better off than the lender, and the lender would therefore adjust the rate he charges to allow for the loss of purchasing power.

All comparisons need to be made on a "level playing field" by bringing all costs to a common point in time, either their present value or a future value some specific years from now.

As an example, the attached table (Exhibit 2-3a) shows the value of the dollar at an annual compounded rate of 6 percent.

In the first column, you can determine what a dollar investment would grow to in the future, e.g., in ten years, the dollar would be worth $1.7908. An investment of $1,000 today would therefore be worth $1,790.80 ten years from now.

In the second column, you can determine what a dollar invested at the end of each year would grow to assuming an annual rate of 6 percent. In ten years, the investment would be worth $13.1807. In other words, an investment of $1,000 at the end of each year would grow to approximately $13,180.70 at the end of ten years.

If you want to know what you have to deposit every year to get one dollar in the future, the third column would permit you to do that. For example, to receive one dollar ten years from now, you would need to invest $0.0758 at the end of every year. To get $1,000 ten years from now, you would need to invest $75.80 per year for ten years.

If you would like to determine the present value of a dollar paid in the future, the fourth column would permit you to calculate it. For example, one dollar paid to you ten years from now is worth only $0.55838. So, the $1,000 you get ten years from now is worth only $558.30 in terms of today's dollars at a discounted annual rate of 6 percent.

Conversely, if you want to know what a future stream of payments is worth today, the fifth column would be what you would need to refer to. So, a dollar paid to you at the end of each year for the next ten years would be worth $7.3600. Therefore, annual payments of $1,000 for the next ten years are worth only $7,360.00 in today's dollars. Let's say a lottery winner wins a prize of a million dollars, payable over twenty years at $50,000 annually. The winner gets $50,000 immediately, and the rest is paid at the end of each year for the next nineteen years. Referring to the table, the true present value of his prize is:

$50,000 for the current payment plus (**$50,000 x 11.1581**)
Or a total of **$607, 905** at an annual interest rate of 6 percent

In other words, the winner is not really a millionaire but something considerably less than that. The amount represents what the winner would get if he took a lump sum calculated at the discounted annual rate of 6 percent. After income taxes reduces the lump sum by another 40 percent, or so, the winner will be left with not even half the amount of the original prize.

This example only utilized an annual rate of 6 percent. You can look up the values for other rates of interest on the Internet.

Exhibit 2-3a
Discounted Cash Flow at 6 Percent/Year

YEARS	Future Value			Present Value	
	What a dollar deposited with Compound Interest will be worth in the future	What a dollar deposited at the end of each period will be worth in the future	What periodic deposit will be worth a dollar at a future date	What a dollar to be paid in the future is worth today	What a dollar to be paid at the end of each period is worth today
1	1.0600	1.0000	1.0000	0.9433	0.9433
2	1.1236	2.0600	0.4854	0.8899	1.8333
3	1.1910	3.1836	0.3141	0.8396	2.6730
4	1.2624	4.3746	0.2285	0.7920	3.4651
5	1.3382	5.6370	0.1773	0.7472	4.2123
10	1.7908	13.1807	0.0758	0.5583	7.3600
15	2.3965	23.2759	0.0429	0.4172	9.7122
19	3.0255	33.7600	0.0296	0.3305	11.1581
20	3.2071	36.7855	0.0271	0.3118	11.4699
25	4.2918	54.8645	0.0182	0.2329	12.7833

Exhibit 2-4
Marginal Tax Bracket vs. Average Tax Rate

Tax Year: **2006**   Filing Status: **Married Filing Jointly**

If Your Taxable Income Is Between...			Your Tax Bracket Is...
0	And	15,100	10%
15,101	And	61,300	15%
61,301	And	123,700	25%
123,701	And	188,450	28%
188,451	And	336,550	33%
336,551	And	above	35%

Your tax bracket is the rate you pay on the "last dollar" you earn, but as a percentage of your income, your average tax rate is generally less than that. To take an example, suppose your taxable income was exactly $100,000 in 2006 and your status was Married Filing Jointly; then, your tax would be calculated like this:

($ 15,100 - 0) x .10:	$1,510
(61,300 - 15,100) x .15:	6,930
(100,000 - 61,300) x .25:	9,675

Total: **$18,115**

This puts you in the 25 percent tax bracket; but, as a percentage of your income, your average tax rate is about 18.12 percent.

Exhibit 2-5
Effects of Inflation

Average U.S. Retail Food Prices
(Bureau of Labor Statistics)

Approx. Cost	A Quart of Milk	A Loaf of White Bread	A Dozen Eggs	A Pound of Round Steak
1941	13.6 cents	8.1 cents	39.7 cents	39.1 cents
1950	20.6 cents	14.3 cents	60.4 cents	93.6 cents
1960	26.0 cents	20.3 cents	57.3 cents	105.5 cents
1970	33.0 cents	24.3 cents	61.4 cents	130.2 cents
1980	52.5 cents	50.9 cents	84.4 cents	276.9 cents
1985	54.1 cents	56.8 cents	90.6 cents	283.4 cents
1990	59.0 cents*	68.6 cents	100.1 cents	342.4 cents
1995	69.0 cents*	83.7 cents	116.0 cents	319.7 cents
2000	89.0 cents*	98.7 cents	95.9 cents	327.8 cents
2005	9.0 cents*	105.5 cents	127.9 cents	393.5 cents

*All statistics provided by Bureau of Labor Statistics (BLS) except ones marked (*), which are based on author's personal experience due to lack of BLS data.

The Consumer Price Index is the government's statistical measure of the changes in prices of goods and services bought by urban wage earners and clerical workers. It is commonly used to measure the **rate of inflation**.

Year	Index	Percent Increase from Previous Year	Purchasing Power of the Dollar
1967 (Base)	100.0	------	$1.00
1970	116.3	5.9%	0.86
1975	161.2	9.1%	0.96
1980	246.8	13.5%	0.96
1985	323.4	3.6%	0.96
1990	391.3	5.4%	0.26
1995	456.3	2.8%	0.22
2000	515.6	3.4%	0.19
2005	591.6	4.6%	0.17

From the table above, we can see that the 1967 dollar is today worth approximately seventeen cents. If you want to determine what today's dollar is in terms of the dollar from a prior year, divide the index for that year by the current index (591.6). For example, to determine how much the dollar's value has dropped due to inflation in twenty years, divide the index for 1985 (323.4) by the current index (538.6) for a value of 0.54. In other words, the dollar has lost 46 percent of its value due to inflation in the past twenty years. Sobering, isn't it? Now you know why inflation is called the "Silent Bandit."

Exhibit 2-6
The Effect of Taxes

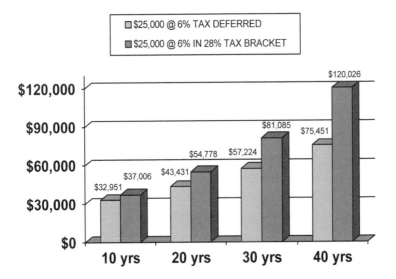

Exhibit 2-7
The Cost of Procrastination

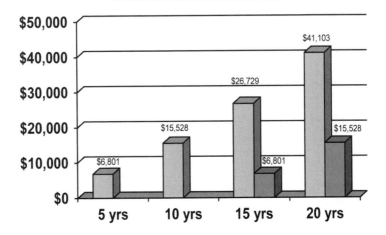

Exhibit 2-8
The Cost of Procrastination

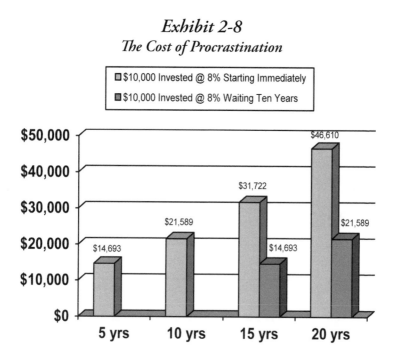

☐ $10,000 Invested @ 8% Starting Immediately
■ $10,000 Invested @ 8% Waiting Ten Years

Exhibit 2-9
The Cost of Procrastination

Obtaining the Million Dollar Retirement Nest Egg by Age Sixty-Five

At age twenty-five (assuming a <u>10 percent</u> annual rate of return), the following combinations will generate a million dollars by age sixty-five:

$	0	lump sum	+	$ 2,055	yearly investment
$	1,000	lump sum	+	$ 1,962	yearly investment
$	2,000	lump sum	+	$ 1,869	yearly investment
$	5,000	lump sum	+	$ 1,590	yearly investment
$	10,000	lump sum	+	$ 1,125	yearly investment
$	15,000	lump sum	+	$ 660	yearly investment
$	22,095	lump sum	+	$ 0	yearly investment

At age thirty-five (assuming a <u>10 percent</u> annual rate of return), the following combinations will generate a million dollars by age sixty-five:

$	0	lump sum	+	$ 5,527	yearly investment
$	5,000	lump sum	+	$ 5,045	yearly investment
$	10,000	lump sum	+	$ 4,563	yearly investment
$	25,000	lump sum	+	$ 3,116	yearly investment
$	35,000	lump sum	+	$ 2,152	yearly investment
$	45,000	lump sum	+	$ 1,187	yearly investment
$	57,309	lump sum	+	$ 0	yearly investment

At age forty-five (assuming a <u>12 percent</u> annual rate of return), the following combinations will generate a million dollars by age sixty-five:

$	0	lump sum	+	$ 12,392	yearly investment
$	5,000	lump sum	+	$ 11,795	yearly investment
$	10,000	lump sum	+	$ 11,197	yearly investment
$	25,000	lump sum	+	$ 9,404	yearly investment
$	50,000	lump sum	+	$ 6,416	yearly investment
$	75,000	lump sum	+	$ 3,427	yearly investment
$	103,667	lump sum	+	$ 0	yearly investment

At age fifty-five (assuming a <u>12 percent</u> annual rate of return), the following combinations will generate a million dollars by age sixty-five:

$ 0	lump sum	+	$ 50,879	yearly investment
$ 50,000	lump sum	+	$ 42,978	yearly investment
$ 75,000	lump sum	+	$ 39,028	yearly investment
$ 100,000	lump sum	+	$ 35,077	yearly investment
$ 200,000	lump sum	+	$ 19,275	yearly investment
$ 250,000	lump sum	+	$ 11,374	yearly investment
$ 321,974	lump sum	+	$ 0	yearly investment

Chapter 3

Finding Out Where You Really Are and Where You Want to Be

TO FIGURE OUT how to get to where you want to go, you have to know where you are.

When it comes to sitting down and doing the work to create your path to Golden Pond, most people stop right here. They agree with the *theory* of getting it all straightened out, and they've probably even read and reread the Eight Great Barriers to Golden Pond, but the next step, finding out where you really are, is one that most people probably won't take.

Why? Simple procrastination (Great Barrier #8). Or, maybe they just do not want to face the truth. As I mentioned previously, there can be a great deal of fear associated with thinking about your money, planning your future, and deciding on how you're going to handle retirement. Most people who've picked up this book aren't feeling completely confident about their future to begin with, and this can cause even more anxiety. So rather than take the chance of feeling even worse when the numbers are actually on the table, they just stop, period.

I'm asking you to take a leap of faith with me.

Work through the next two chapters. Give it your undivided attention. It's not going to be as overwhelming or glum as you may expect. And, at the end of these two chapters, I can guarantee that you'll have a much-improved outlook and mood about your future. **The key is taking control of your life**, and these two chapters help you do exactly that.

The Income (Cash Flow) Statement: "**Happiness is positive cash flow.**"

You will need to figure out where your money is coming from, where your money is going, and how much. The objective is to be able to complete the Income Statement (**Exhibit 3-1**), but you can come up with your own version as long as it has the necessary details.

Your prior year's tax returns, your check books, your money market statements, your credit card bills, and your paycheck stub will all be useful in the preparation of this form, so make sure you have access to all of these documents. The purpose of this form is to determine your cash flow.

You will need to take a few moments to figure out your different sources of income. Usually this doesn't take long. These sources include salary, interest, dividends, rental income, pensions, annuities, social security, etc. Most people can put together their total annual income and its sources in a few minutes. You can enter the amounts directly on to **Exhibit 3-1**.

Expenses are a little tougher to arrive at than income, and therefore they take a little longer. There are many categories of expenses. Also, some of these expenses occur at different frequencies. For example, rent might be monthly, property taxes might be semi-annually, transportation might be daily, food could be daily or weekly, while insurance might be an annual expense. All of these expenses need to be annualized to come up with **annual** expenses. To simplify the matter, you should complete the "Details of Annual Expenses" worksheet (**Exhibit 3-2**) prior to entering the expenses on the Income Statement.

You can handle income taxes in two different ways:
1. You can take income tax withholding on your paycheck stub as an expense. If you do that, you will need to consider the refund you get (if any) as a source of income. Or, if you had to pay additional taxes on April 15th, then you have to add that additional tax to the amount you obtained from the paycheck stubs.

2. The second method is to ignore the paycheck stubs and get the total tax information directly from the tax returns. This method could result in a time lag because tax returns are not prepared until we are well into the next year.

I usually prefer to use the first method. I believe it is a little more accurate. However, either one is fine as long as you can figure out just how much goes to federal, state, and local income taxes, withholdings for Social Security and Medicare, as well as deductions for benefits such as life insurance, long-term disability insurance, 401(k) contributions, etc. (note: your last paycheck stub for the year has all the information neatly summarized for you). The Balance Sheet (net worth statement, **Exhibit 3-3**) lists all your assets (what you own) and your liabilities (what you owe). The difference between the two is your net worth, and that tells you how well off you are. Keeping track of net worth is extremely critical as you make your way towards Golden Pond. Just as a doctor uses a thermometer to measure your temperature and determine your medical health, net worth is an indicator of your financial health. If you want to get to Golden Pond, the net worth has got to keep increasing over time. And if by chance that number is negative or is declining annually, some action needs to be taken ... *fast!*

Your Assets

In completing the balance sheet, you will need to make educated guesses about the various assets you own. Try not to exaggerate. It serves no useful purpose (yes, I know it might make you feel good, but you know the truth, so who are you fooling, anyway?) In fact, it's a very good idea to *underestimate* the values. For example, you may feel your house is worth $300,000, but if you had to sell it in a hurry, you might only get, say, $290,000. The Realtor's commissions would also eat into the price you get. So instead of $300,000, I might be more inclined to put down $280,000. But DON'T put down $325,000 just so you feel good about yourself. You would be doing yourself a big disservice. **Remember, the value of something is what someone is willing to pay for it, not what you want for it.**

It should be mentioned that **Exhibit 3-3** is just one, very simplistic example of a balance sheet. There are other ways to classify assets and liabilities. For example, CPAs and accountants would classify assets into the following three separate categories:

- **Liquid**: these are assets you can liquidate right away to raise cash. These are items such as checking and savings accounts, money market funds; stocks, bonds, and other investments in your taxable (non-IRA) accounts. The values of these items are readily available and you can be fairly certain of getting that value if you were to liquidate those assets today.

- **Tax-deferred** - these are assets such as the investments in your IRAs, 401(k)s and other such types of accounts that are not taxed for now. You cannot get your hands on these until you reach a certain age, usually fifty-nine and a half. Tax on the growth in these accounts is deferred until you take the money out of these accounts (note: you could withdraw funds from the IRA before fifty nine and a half by paying a penalty or under certain conditions). For the purposes of this exercise, let's just say that these are assets that are off limits until you are at least fifty nine and a half years old.

- **Illiquid** - sometimes called "fixed assets." Selling these assets takes time; therefore, they are considered illiquid. Real estate is one example. Plus, you are not certain of the exact amount or the exact time it would take to get your hands on the proceeds of the sale. However, you should enter the estimated current market value of these assets for now.

Your Liabilities

For this, list all your debts—credit card balances, outstanding balances on your mortgage, car loans, and any other loans that are outstanding. When you add these up, you have your Total Liabilities. Again, **Exhibit 3-3** is just an example. CPAs and accountants would want to break down the liabilities into two separate categories: **Short-Term**: loans and payments that are due within the next twelve months. **Long-Term**: loans that are due beyond twelve months. I do not want to intimidate you. Nor do I want to make accountants out of you. So for all intents and purposes, the classifications shown in **Exhibit 3-3** will suit us just fine.

Your Net Worth

This is the amount you get when you subtract the Total Liabilities from your Total Assets. **This is the most important indicator of your financial health**. It tells you how well or how badly off you are. As I stated before, by keeping track of your Net Worth periodically, you will be able to determine if you are making any progress toward Golden Pond. The obvious way to increase your net worth is to grow your assets and keep your liabilities as low as possible; or better yet, decrease or eliminate them.

I am usually asked by the attendees at seminars what would be a "good" net worth to shoot for. Unfortunately, there is no one right answer. I am not trying to avoid answering this question, but the number is totally dependent upon your own individual circumstances and what retirement lifestyle you desire. What one person considers adequate could be considered totally inadequate by another. In general, though, the higher the number, the better off you are.

Where Do You Want To Be? When?

Okay, now that we have figured out where we are, it's time to take a look at our goals and objectives. What is it you are trying to accomplish? Just exactly what does your Golden Pond mean to you in dollars and cents?

No matter which way you look at it, there are only so many things people want to do with their lives. For sure, *the* main focus is on retirement. Let's say you never want to retire. That's fine, too. So, instead of the word "retirement," let's call it "financial independence." As a reminder, that's the stage of your life when you don't have to work for a living if you don't want to. So, at what age and with how many dollars per month would you consider yourself financially independent?

First, let's decide on the age at which you want to be financially independent. **Remember, the earlier you retire, the longer the period of time you will need to provide for with the nest egg**

you are trying to build. For example, if you want to quit work at fifty-five years of age, you may need to provide for perhaps another forty years of life.

Yes, Social Security will offset the load a bit, but it will be several years before those payments kick in. So you may need to provide for an additional amount in the first years of your retired life to allow for the fact that Social Security benefits will not begin until at least ten years later and perhaps as many as twenty, depending on just how early you want to call it quits. Moreover, we have no way of knowing how those benefits may change going out to the year 2026 and beyond.

Note: There is a lot of controversy over whether the social security system will even be around by the time some of us retire. While it is almost certain that some form of social security will be around for a long time, I believe it is a good idea to not even consider it as a potential source of income during retirement. In other words, don't even take it into account. This is a conservative approach to planning for your retired life and might even require you to save more than you would like to during your earning years, but it might pay off for you in the long run. If social security payments are not forthcoming when you retire, or are not as much as you originally anticipated, your foresight will have prevented you from finding yourself "up the creek." If payments do materialize, then those extra savings will be icing on the cake, and you will be able to live an even better life on your Golden Pond.

Okay, so now you have decided **when** you are going to retire. It's now time to figure out **how much** money you will need at retirement. Take a good, long, and hard look at your expenses and come up with a figure (in today's dollars) that you would be able to live comfortably on. Some people take the easy way out and say they want to maintain their current lifestyle and might decide that that is the amount they would like to have. Certainly that's as good an approach as any. But, surely your retirement objectives deserve a bit more of your time than just a "seat of the pants" figure that you arrive at in five seconds.

Before you finalize a dollar amount, keep in mind that at retirement you probably will have paid off your house. Also, you may be spending more on items such as medical costs, travel, etc., while you may decrease your spending on clothing, commuting, etc. Usually, I have found that after some thought, people come up with income needs that match about 75–80 percent of their pre-retirement monthly expenses. In some cases, in the initial stages of retirement, it is entirely possible that your needs might be 110 percent or even 120 percent of your current monthly expenses. That's fine. There's nothing wrong with that as long as you have planned for it. In most cases, though, I have found that as people grow older and less mobile, they tend to spend much less on discretionary items and grow increasingly conservative. Every case is unique, and your requirements will be totally different from those of your brother, friend, or colleague. It is therefore not a good idea to utilize some arbitrary rule of thumb such as "80 percent of my current monthly expenses" based on what you saw in a magazine or on the internet. It is imperative that **you** figure out what **your** needs are going to be so you can start making plans for **your own** Golden Pond. You can complete the worksheet **(Exhibit 3-4)** to help you decide just how much you need to live on during retirement.

This form is almost the same as **Exhibit 3-2,** and you should have no problem completing it. You will need to review this form in Chapter 5. It will, however, involve some thinking on your part. Thinking can be painful, I know. But hey, this form tells us what it would take to live **On Golden Pond**, and for that reason alone, it's well worth the effort.

After you have completed the analysis of your needs, you may wish to put down your retirement objective on the Golden Pond Objectives Worksheet **(Exhibit 3-5)**, along with other objectives we will now discuss.

Okay, we have retirement out of the way. Let's see what else we will need to plan for as we make our way to Golden Pond - items that could blindside us and derail our plans. College education and your children's weddings may need to be budgeted, planned, and saved for. Let's start with college education for your children. You will have to decide whether your children will be going to a community college, an in-state or out-of-state university, or a private university. In 2006, the yearly college costs could easily vary from about $8,000 per year to almost $50,000 per year! Multiply that by four years and you have a range of $8,000 to $200,000 *in terms of today's dollars.* Now factor in an inflation factor of 8 percent. By the "Rule of 72," that means college costs could double every nine years. So, if you have a child today and the baby is going to college in eighteen years, keep in mind that college costs could double twice by the time he or she enters college. In the above case, **the range for a four-year college education could be $128,000 to $800,000!** Okay, pick yourself up from the floor. It really is not as bad as the numbers indicate, and there is some college planning that needs to be done.

Once the decision is made as to which college you want to plan for, you will need to decide just how much you want to contribute toward your child's college education… 20 percent? 50 percent? 100 percent? 0 percent? Will he qualify for scholarships? Will he be able to work part-time to offset some of the costs? Will he need to take out a loan? There is nothing wrong with admitting that, much as you would like to, you cannot afford to pay 100 percent of your children's college costs—especially if it means jeopardizing your own ability to be self-sufficient and financially secure during your retirement years! I have seen countless cases where parents have worked two jobs to be able to send their children to college. They compromised their own financial health only to have their children not even acknowledge their existence after they graduated and started earning a decent salary. Are you banking on the fact that your children will help you out financially after they start making a decent salary? Forget about it! I know it might be controversial, but I believe **your retirement security should take precedence over your children's college education.**

There is no doubt that your children's marriages are a major milestone in your lives. However, these can also burn a huge hole in your pocket if you allow them to. Just how much do you intend to pay for your child's wedding? All of it? Part of it? A fixed amount? Just how much?

Unlike college education, one cannot tell with any kind of certainty when the children will get married. It is therefore best to plan for an earlier wedding than a later one. Granted, that might mean you have to save more than you want to because of the shorter time frame, but a conservative approach works best. If he or she gets married later than you planned for, there is no harm done. However, if you planned for a later wedding and the reverse happens to be the case, you just might find yourself a little under-funded when the big day actually arrives.

In helping my clients with their retirement goals and objectives, one item usually does crop up on their "wish list": a big trip or a vacation after retirement. If that's the case with you, just consider it as an expense similar to your child's wedding. Put it down on the list of your retirement objectives, along with the anticipated date for such an event.

In addition to your needs pertaining to retirement, college education, weddings, and other special events, you may also have other objectives. This could involve the downsizing of your current home, or purchasing a second home in a warmer climate. All of these could be classified as "special events" and need to be included on the worksheet.

At this point, it would be interesting to review and complete **Exhibit 3-6**. This is perhaps the best of all the exhibits because it can keep you from going berserk with your frivolous expenses. **In fact, you should plan to complete this worksheet to determine if / when you might run out of your resources.** In the example provided in **Exhibit 3-6a**, the individual will run out of money in fifteen years. Whether that's good or bad depends on the circumstances of that individual.

Let's see where you stand right now, okay? You have identified the Eight Great Barriers to Golden Pond, and, through awareness of those barriers, you have promised yourself not to fall victim to any of them. Great!

You then created a complete list of your income and expenses for getting to and staying on Golden Pond. You listed your assets and liabilities, and now you know your "net worth." You also identified a list of life events you need to plan for on your way to Golden Pond. You have also been able to figure out exactly how long your resources will last.

By now, I am sure you feel more empowered than you have ever felt about your finances and can begin to see the "big picture." For once, you should feel that you are making some progress in your efforts to take control of your financial life. Don't lose this feeling, because in the next chapter you will need to go a step further and analyze the data you have accumulated and summarized.

Exhibit 3-1
Income Statement:

ANNUAL ESTIMATES

GROSS INCOME	Now	At Retirement
Salary, Wages, Tips		
Business Income		
Interest & Dividends		
Rent/Royalty Income		
Pension Income		
Social Security		
A. GROSS INCOME		

NET INCOME		
B. TOTAL LIVING EXPENSES (from Exhibits 3-2 & 3-4)		
C. NET INCOME (A minus B)		

OTHER		
D. TOTAL OTHER CASH REQUIREMENTS		

NET CASH FLOW		
E. NET CASH FLOW (C minus D)		

Exhibit 3-2
Details of Projected Annual Expenses

PERIODIC_____ **REGULAR**_____

	Column 1 MONTHLY	Column 2 QUARTERLY	Column 3 SEMI-ANNUALLY	Column 4 ANNUALLY
FIXED				
Taxes				
• Federal				
• State				
• Local				
• Social Security				
• Medicare				
Housing				
• Rent/Mortgage				
• Property Taxes				
• Utilities				
• Repairs/ Maintenance				
Transportation				
• Auto Payment(s)				
• Auto Insurance				
• Gas				
• Repairs/ Maintenance				
• Licenses				
• Tolls				
• Commuting				
Insurance				
• Life				
• Medical/Dental				
• Disability				
• Long Term Care				
Education				
• Child Care				
• School/College				
Credit Card Payments				
•				
•				
•				
Other				
•				
•				
•				
•				
•				
•				

DISCRETIONARY				
Personal				
• Food				
• Misc. Household Needs				
• Personal Grooming				
• Gifts				
• Donations				
• Furniture & Furnishings				
• Clothing				
• Entertainment				
• Vacations				
• Cable TV				
• Club Dues/ Recreation				
Other				
•				
•				
•				
TOTAL LIVING EXPENSES (A)				
Multiplier (B) to convert to Annual Expense	12	4	2	1
(A) X (B)	_____ + _____ + _____ + _____			
TOTAL ANNUAL LIVING EXPENSES	$ _____			

Exhibit 3-3
Net Worth Statement (Balance Sheet)

ASSETS	
Cash and Cash Equivalents	$ _____
Invested Assets	
Insurance and Annuities	$ _____
Stocks, Mutual Funds	$ _____
Bonds, Mutual Funds	$ _____
Partnerships	$ _____
Real Estate	$ _____
Notes and Trust Deeds	$ _____
Other Assets	$ _____
Total Invested Assets	$ _____
Personal Assets	$ _____
Furnishings	$ _____
Automobiles	$ _____
Recreational Vehicles	$ _____
Collections	$ _____
Other	$ _____
Total Personal Assets	$ _____
TOTAL ASSETS	$ _____

LIABILITIES

Secured Liabilities

Mortgage on Residence	$ _____
Other Mortgages	$ _____
Automobile Loans	$ _____
Notes and Trust Deeds	$ _____
Loans Against Life Insurance	$ _____
Other	$ _____
Total Secured Liabilities	$ _____

Unsecured Liabilities

Credit Cards	$ _____
Bills Due	$ _____
Personal Loans	$ _____
Other	$ _____
Total Unsecured Liabilities	$ _____
TOTAL ASSETS	$ _____

TOTAL ASSETS $ _____
– TOTAL LIABILITIES $ _____
= TOTAL NET WORTH $ _____

Exhibit 3-4
Estimated Expenses at Retirement

PERIODIC_____   REGULAR_____

	Column 1 MONTHLY	Column 2 QUARTERLY	Column 3 SEMI-ANNUALLY	Column 4 ANNUALLY
FIXED:				
Taxes				
• Federal				
• State				
• Local				
• Social Security				
• Medicare				
Housing				
• Rent/Mortgage				
• Property Taxes				
• Utilities				
• Repairs/ Maintenance				
Transportation				
• Auto Payment(s)				
• Auto Insurance				
• Gas				
• Repairs/ Maintenance				
• Licenses				
• Tolls				
• Commuting				
Insurance				
• Life				
• Medical/Dental				
• Disability				
• Long Term Care				
Education				
• Child Care				
• School/College				
Credit Card Payments				
•				
•				
•				
Other				
•				
•				
•				
•				
•				
•				

DISCRETIONARY				
Personal				
• Food				
• Misc. Household Needs				
• Personal Grooming				
• Gifts				
• Donations				
• Furniture & Furnishings				
• Clothing				
• Entertainment				
• Vacations				
• Cable TV				
• Club Dues/ Recreation				
Other				
•				
•				
•				
TOTAL LIVING EXPENSES (A)				
Multiplier (B) to convert to Annual Expense	12	4	2	1
(A) X (B)				
	_____ + _____ + _____ + _____			
TOTAL ANNUAL LIVING EXPENSES AT RETIREMENT	$ _____			

Exhibit 3-5
Golden Pond Objectives

• RETIREMENT:

I wish to be financially independent by the date __/__/__ with $_____
per month in today's dollars.

• COLLEGE EDUCATION:

Name of Child	Year College Begins	Estimated Cost (Today's dollars)
_____	_____	_____
_____	_____	_____
_____	_____	_____
_____	_____	_____

• CHILDREN'S WEDDINGS:

Name of Child	Date of Wedding	Estimated Cost (Today's dollars)
_____	_____	_____
_____	_____	_____
_____	_____	_____
_____	_____	_____

• SPECIAL EVENTS:

Name of Child	Date of Event	Estimated Cost (Today's dollars)
_____	_____	_____
_____	_____	_____
_____	_____	_____
_____	_____	_____

Exhibit 3-6
How Much Income Will Your Retirement Savings Produce?

1. **Amount Currently in Retirement Savings**
   (Income Producing Assets)

   $ _____

2. **Income Needed to Live Desired Lifestyle**
   (Annually)

   $ _____

3. **Fixed Sources of Annual Retirement Income:**

   Pension   _____

   Social Security   _____

   Other   _____   _____

Total Fixed Income $ _____

4. **Balance Which Must Come from Retirement Savings** $ _____

5. **Withdrawal from Retirement Savings as a Percentage of the Entire Fund**

   Line 4 _____ / Line 1 _____ = _____ %

6. **Assumed Average Rate of Return on the Fund**   _____ %

Exhibit 3-6a
How Long the Retirement Savings Will Last

Circle the % On Line 5 ⬇	Percentage Rate of Return on Investment – (Circle the % on Line 6)											
	5	6	7	8	9	10	11	12	13	14	15	16
25	4	5	5	5	5	5	5	5	6	6	6	6
24	5	5	5	5	5	5	6	6	6	6	7	7
23	5	5	5	5	6	6	6	6	6	7	7	8
22	5	5	5	6	6	6	6	7	7	7	8	8
21	5	6	6	6	6	7	7	7	7	8	8	9
20	6	6	6	6	7	7	7	8	8	8	9	10
19	6	6	7	7	7	8	8	8	9	10	11	12
18	7	7	7	7	8	8	9	9	10	11	12	14
17	7	7	8	8	9	9	10	10	11	12	15	18
16	8	8	8	9	9	10	11	12	13	15	19	
15	8	9	9	9	10	11	12	14	16	20		
14	9	9	10	10	11	13	14	17	21			
13	10	10	11	11	13	15	17	22				
12	11	12	12	14	16	18	23					
11	12	13	14	16	19	25						
10	14	15	17	20	26							
9	16	18	22	28								
8	20	23	30									
7	25	33										
6	36											

(Left vertical label: Percentage Rate of Withdrawal (Line 5))

Capital Would Not Be Consumed in this Lower Area, Because the Annual Return Exceeds Annual Rate of Withdrawl

The place where the row and the column intersect indicates the number of years the capital will last.

For example, if your rate of return is 6 percent and your withdrawal rate is 10 percent per year, your Nest Egg will last fifteen years.

Chapter 4

Taking Control!

Why Managing Your Money Today Creates Your Golden Pond of Tomorrow

NO MATTER HOW rich or well-off people are, each and every one of us wants more. I have no doubt that you're of the same opinion. In order to create more, you've simply got to become the business manager of every dime that marches through your door.

People make a big deal out of the management of money, like it's a mysterious and complicated alchemy that requires all of your attention and focus. In actuality, the secret of great money management lies in just five words...to repeat what I said in Chapter 2: **Spend less than you make.** There. Five words and this chapter is done. Honestly, that's all there is to managing money. Most people simply don't want to monitor what they spend, much less adjust accordingly. But if you're going to increase inflow and decrease outflow, it's time to get a handle on your income and your spending habits. The worksheet you prepared in the previous chapter (**Exhibit 3-1**) should help you to get that handle.

Sometimes increasing cash flow could be just a matter of adjusting your tax withholding from your paycheck. If you find that you get big refunds every year from the federal or state authorities, you are being over-withheld. You could opt to reduce the withholding and increase the amount you receive each pay period.

However, it's usually not that simple. But, it's not that complicated either. Many people out there think they've got to do something really **big** in order to increase inflow. As an example, many come to the conclusion that they need to pursue a higher-paying job. This may or may not involve more education. While a higher-paying job will certainly do the trick of increasing inflow, it takes a while to see the fruits of your labor and sacrifice. You could also get a second job. You could invest in assets that produce a higher return. Heck, you could even marry a rich person and all of your problems would be over, right? Maybe. Maybe not. In reality, even if one of the aforementioned moves panned out, they would still require time.

So, while you are out there waiting for that higher-paying job, or Mister (or Miss) Megabucks to show up and sweep you off your feet, there are a few other cost-cutting measures that you could undertake—measures that will help you here and now.

There are some of you out there who, no matter what you earn, are always going to live beyond your means. For those "spendaholics," before you go out to get a higher paying job, it would be an extremely good idea to figure out where you can cut expenses. **Cutting expenses is the equivalent of getting a higher income**. After all, a penny saved is a penny earned, right?

Analyzing Your Current Situation:

So, let's have a reality check and see exactly where you stand in terms of income, expenses, and net worth by reviewing your Income Statement (**Exhibit 3-1**) and Annual Expenses Worksheet (**Exhibit 3-2**).

If you find that you have zero or negative cash flow, you should stop right here. You have just found out that your expenses are either equal to your income or, worse, your expenses exceed your income. Even people who find that they have positive cash flow can benefit from the following exercise. Go over your expenses very carefully and determine where you may be able to cut them down. Do you really need cable TV? Do you really need to spend $5,000 on a one-week vacation? Do you really need to eat at a fancy restaurant every weekend? Why not drop your daily cup of coffee to an every-other-day cup of coffee? Or, if you are a smoker, why not cut out cigarettes? Now, that's quite a mind shift, isn't it? Truth is, most people fritter away their long-term future on small expenditures here and there throughout their day. You pick up your daily coffee and a newspaper. You may hit a vending machine later, or go out for a quick sandwich, or buy a lottery ticket. You pick up a couple of things at the store on the way home, regardless of your refrigerator's current contents. If you choose, instead, to consciously do without just one item each day, those three or five dollars can grow into a sizeable sum thanks to the magic of compound interest, which pays interest and then earns interest on that interest. The longer your money is invested, the more compound interest works for you.

Saving just three dollars a day adds ups to $1,095 in one year. Invest $1,095 per year at 8 percent for twenty-five years, and you'll have more than $80,000. Not too shabby!

You will find that you are able to reduce your expenses considerably as a result of reviewing your expenses and asking yourself hard questions, such as *"Do I really need this item?"* or *"Do I really need to spend so much on this item?"* The object of this exercise is to wind up with 10 to 25 percent of your Disposable Income on the Net Cash Flow line.

Note: A great way to come up with the savings is to develop a **PRIORITIZED** list of expenses for the month. Mortgage/rent would be a very high priority, as are food, auto, etc. But right up there with all the other priorities should be the category "Golden Pond" (See **Exhibit 4-1).** Many people spend a lot of money on items they believe have a higher priority than retirement. If there is anything left over, they use that to fund their retirement nest egg (and sometimes, their children's college education). Guess what? **In**

most cases, there isn't anything left over to put away. And even if there was, the money that was saved will most likely be spent on a "**whim du jour.**"

Folks, if you are serious about saving for retirement, you **have** to give it a higher priority and make do without some other frivolous expenses (e.g. dining out, cable TV, movies). You **have** to budget some money to the "Golden Pond" category. Once it is funded, consider it off-limits except for dire emergencies. The object is not to do without the things that you enjoy in life, but to make sure some of your retirement security priorities are addressed before you go and splurge on the fun things in life.

After you have tried everything you possibly can to reduce your expenses, and you find you still cannot save or invest any money each month, it is time to face reality and admit that you will never wind up on Golden Pond unless you take extreme measures to increase your income. This might mean getting more education, more specialized training, switching jobs, or perhaps even switching careers.

One warning: There are a lot of people out there who spend like they are the United States Government. They believe in deficit spending; i.e. they spend with the expectation that in the future, a higher income will take care of their expenses and debt. This is a very dangerous game and can only lead to financial disaster. Unlike the government, you cannot print more money to get you out of a bind. Take it from me, once you get used to living beyond your means it will be almost impossible to cut back. In other words, like a drug addict, once you start spending, you are hooked! *Never, ever spend more than you make*. If you do, it will come back to haunt you one day; I guarantee it!

Now that you have analyzed your Income Statement and Annual Expense Worksheet, it is time to look at your Balance Sheet (**Exhibit 3-3**). If you find that your Net Worth is a negative amount and your liabilities exceed your assets, then you are "in the hole" by that amount. The biggest culprit is probably your debt. If this is the case, you will have to start paying down the debt before you can even think about starting to make any headway toward your Golden Pond. You will have to resolve that **while you are in**

the process of paying down the debt and becoming solvent, you will not purchase any items on credit or with money you do not have. In fact, I know several people who found themselves "Up The Creek" and decided to go "cold turkey." They tore up all their credit cards just to avoid any future temptation. Now that is what I call commitment!

For your Net Worth to be positive and increase in the right direction, your assets have to go up and your liabilities have to come down. Here is an important lesson: if you are serious about increasing your net worth, some parts of your income have to be allocated to one of the three categories of assets listed above —saving, investing, home, etc. In other words, your cash outflow must move toward increasing your assets or reducing your debt (See **Exhibit 4**-2). Moreover, these assets should be growing in value. Unfortunately, cars are an asset, but they do not grow in value. However, they are what I consider a necessary evil, and we just have to learn to minimize their impact. By the same token, when you go out and splurge on something that is not all that critical and you cannot afford it anyway because you don't have the money, you charge it and wind up increasing your debt. This, in turn, increases your liabilities, and reduces your Net Worth. I realize a person has to live, so I have taken items such as food into serious consideration as an expense, and they do not affect your net worth. However, there must be a balance between your current enjoyment and your future security. It is never a good strategy to emphasize one at the expense of another. Keep in mind that every dollar wasted is a dollar that could have increased your net worth.

This is where the power of investing can really help you. Let's say you spend $1,000 of your income on an investment, and after a few years it is worth $11,000. Your cash outflow of $1,000 has improved your net worth by $10,000! That's great! Congratulations. This is truly the secret behind building your net worth and by extension, your wealth. However, if you invest $1,000 in a pie-in-the sky scheme and wind up losing the entire investment, you have just set your net worth back by $1,000. Similarly, the wise use of borrowing to invest (e.g. your own home) is a great move and you can leverage your own net worth with the use of the lender's money. However, borrowing money to invest in a risky scheme where you could lose it all would be calamitous to your net worth and your plans for retirement security. Perhaps a better plan would be to sock it away for a rainy day

It is time to go back to the "liquid" assets section of the Balance Sheet. This is the sum of your savings, checking accounts, and money market accounts. Not all of this money should be invested in stocks, bonds, etc. This account should have perhaps three to six months of your monthly expenses in it. This amount could be referred to as "Emergency Reserves." If only one spouse is working, the reserve should be as high as three to six months' working capital (depending on your comfort level); whereas if both spouses are employed, the reserve could be as low as two to three months' working capital. This amount can be tapped into in the event of a catastrophe, such as the loss of the breadwinner's job, home repairs, etc., so that you do not wind up liquidating your investments at an inopportune time.

Once the emergency reserves have been set aside, all of the balance of the liquid assets should be put to use in investments that generate a higher rate of return than what the liquid assets earn. I realize the stock market was not kind to investors between 2000 and 2002, but with proper diversification and asset allocation, among various asset classes, you should be able to minimize your risk and achieve returns that are two to four times the return that you can currently get from a money market or savings account.

A budget doesn't have to be a bad thing It is truly the mechanism for helping you "spend less than you make." Setting up a budget may seem tedious and dull, but it's the bedrock to building your financial future. As you set up a realistic budget that covers day-to-day expenses and your long-term needs, you'll need to track where your money goes initially. This will allow you to cut back more easily on expenses. It also gives you insight into the type of spender you are.

Big spenders can't resist spending and often carry credit card debt. If you're one such spender, set up auto-deposits from your paycheck to accounts you don't touch. It's a simple and first solution.

Non-spenders are those frugal people who are certainly admirable as long as their penny-pinching habits do not prevent them from enjoying life. As an example, I know a man (not a client) who's a whiz at saving and investing money. He feels ready to get married and sees himself as a perfect catch to any husband-seeking woman. Unfortunately, he lives in a rundown house, has no dishwasher or clothes dryer, and drives a car whose passenger-side door doesn't even open. Now, I'm not saying the "perfect catch" of a bachelor has a 6,000 square-foot modern home and drives a BMW, but this type of frugality may be a bit disconcerting to the average American woman. **Don't let your frugality get in the way of your happiness or comfort**.

Sloppy spenders never balance their checkbooks or keep track of the amounts that were charged on their credit cards. They don't know where their money goes, they rarely double-check their bills before paying, and they couldn't tell you how much they have in their bank account. Imagine how much better off this sloppy spender would be if he were to simply begin organizing his financial records and reviewing his spending habits.

Okay, let's see where we stand now. You have identified where your money goes, and you have decided to "trim the fat" from your expenses by identifying inefficient spending behavior in your day-to-day life. You are now at a point where your expenses are finally less than your income. You have also reviewed your use of credit cards and have taken measures to ensure that they become less of an intrusion in your life. Let's go out and celebrate the occasion at an expensive French restaurant. Hey, come back! You have to resist the urge to do that. It will undo what you have struggled so hard to do. It's like working out at a health club for two hours and then rewarding yourself with a big, high-calorie meal. While some form of reward for your efforts is a good idea, *you have to resist the urge to splurge*. Your ability to reach Golden Pond depends on it!

Make room in your budget to start paying well over the minimum amounts on your outstanding loan payments. If you do not have a positive net worth, you should start making headway soon with proper investing of your surplus cash flow.

Note: since we are discussing credit cards, now would be an excellent time to **run a credit report on yourself.** In addition to discovering inaccuracies, you may be able to find out just how credit-worthy you really are. Your credit worthiness is reflected by your credit score, which can range from zero to over eight hundred. Scores above seven hundred reflect good credit, while scores below five hundred reflect poor credit. If your credit rating is such that you would not be able to get a loan, that should tell you something about your financial situation.

At this point you should have a fairly good handle on your finances. If you are mathematically challenged, or just do not have the time or the inclination to proceed further with some math (discounted cash flow) calculations (see Exhibits 2-3 and 2-3a), you can engage the services of a professional who can do it for you. I show you how to do that in Chapter 10. The data you have gathered so far should prove to be of tremendous value to you, as well as the advisor, and may even result in some reduction of the fees involved.

Or, you can attempt to do this on your own. However, I suggest you read through the entire book before you tackle the project. Once you have read the book and begun to understand the entire process of planning for your retirement security, you can refer to the above-mentioned exhibits. You should also refer to Exhibit 4-3 to get a better understanding of the calculations that may be involved as you attempt to determine what it would take to reach your Golden Pond. If you are unsure of your calculations, you can hire a professional to validate the numbers for you. This should not cost a lot, but the trick will be in finding a professional who will agree to take on such a minor project. Many advisors typically like to develop long-term relationships with clients rather than deal with "one and done"–type customers.

If you want, you can also utilize "financial calculators" that are readily available on the websites of various financial institutions, perhaps including the provider of 401(k) services at you place of employment. These may provide the answers for you. However, it is better for you to understand how those numbers are derived, so some knowledge of the calculations shown in Exhibit 4-3 is truly advisable.

It is not really important HOW you complete the planning process—you can do it with or without the assistance of a professional, or you can use the internet or whatever means you have at your disposal. It is, however, extremely important that you do complete the process. There is just too much at stake, and you have a lot to lose. Remember, it's your entire retirement (spanning 30 to 40 years!) we are talking about here. You HAVE to get it done. For the sake of your own peace of mind and to improve your chances of achieving your ultimate objective (i.e. Golden Pond), don't let Great Barrier #8 (procrastination) mentioned in Chapter 2 get you. Don't keep putting it off. You have worked too hard to get to where you are to let this barrier stand in your way now.

So let's keep paddling, shall we? You are well on your way to Golden Pond.

Exhibit 4-1
Funding for Golden Pond

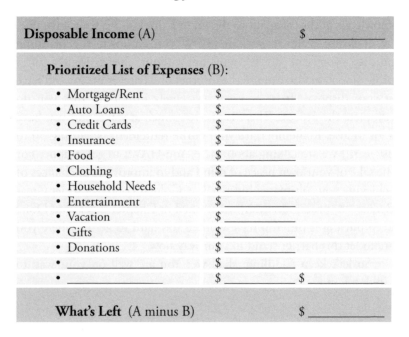

Disposable Income (A) $ _____

Prioritized List of Expenses (B):

- Mortgage/Rent $ _____
- Auto Loans $ _____
- Credit Cards $ _____
- Insurance $ _____
- Food $ _____
- Clothing $ _____
- Household Needs $ _____
- Entertainment $ _____
- Vacation $ _____
- Gifts $ _____
- Donations $ _____
- _____ $ _____
- _____ $ _____ $ _____

What's Left (A minus B) $ _____

Is "What's Left" funding your Golden Pond objectives? Are you relying on "What's Left" to provide for your children's college education? Your daughter's wedding? Your own retirement? If so, you need to assign a much higher priority to those specific objectives.

Suggestion: Golden Pond (Retirement), College, and Weddings should have higher priority than Entertainment and Vacation. All expenses need to be carefully examined to determine the possibility of reducing or eliminating them.

Exhibit 4-2
Spending and Net Worth

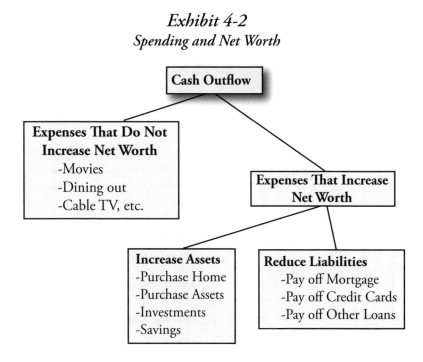

Exhibit 4-3
Sample Calculations for Retirement

(Note: These calculations merely illustrate the process and are not intended to be comprehensive.)

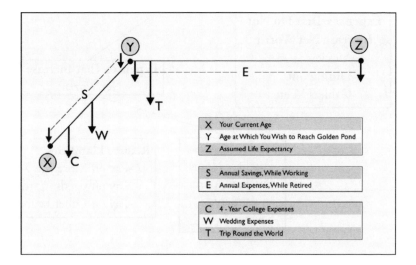

X	Your Current Age
Y	Age at Which You Wish to Reach Golden Pond
Z	Assumed Life Expectancy

S	Annual Savings, While Working
E	Annual Expenses, While Retired

C	4 - Year College Expenses
W	Wedding Expenses
T	Trip Round the World

College Education: How much do you need to save per year to be able to provide for "C"—your child's four-year college education? (Future Value of monthly or annual payments at a specified rate of return for a specified time.) Or, how much do you need to have saved right now (at Point "X" on the chart) so that you can afford to pay for four years of college education ("C") in the future? (Present Value of four years of college expenses at a specified time in the future.) If you have more than one child, you will have to repeat the calculations for each to come up with composite totals for college education.

Wedding: Same calculations as for college education

Retirement:

1. How much money will your monthly or annual savings ("S") amount to at retirement (Point "Y" on the chart), taking into account "C" and "W" for the children? (Similar to Future Value calculation for College Education.)

2. How much money will you need at Retirement (Point "Y" on the chart) to be able to spend a specific amount ("E") every year, taking into account a specified rate of inflation? (Present Value of a stream of monthly or annual expenditures at a specified rate of inflation.) Also, what is the present value of the "Round the World Trip" (Point "Y" on the chart) at retirement?

3. If the total from 1) is greater than the total from 2) at retirement (Point "Y" on the chart), then you have a good chance of getting to your Golden Pond and staying there.

4. If the total from 1) is less than the total from 2) at retirement (Point "Y" on the chart), you have a shortfall. That shortfall needs to be made up by increasing your savings or reducing your expenses during retirement. Once you decide to do either one, you have to repeat steps 1) and 2) until you achieve the desired result.

Chapter 5

The "Evil Twins": Inflation and Taxes

OKAY, SO YOU'VE decided on **when** you want to be financially independent. You've also decided on **how much** money per month you need to be financially independent. Furthermore, you figured out how much you should set aside in order to live the lifestyle you desire.

On the surface, all of this stuff may look quite plain and ordinary—it looks like you will be able to make it to Golden Pond after all. But there are two evil twins lurking in the background and, if you don't watch out, they could wreak havoc with your finances. If you have not paid attention to inflation and income taxes, and if you don't start paying attention now, you could find out too late that you are "Up The Creek," or at the very least, that the estimated time of arrival on Golden Pond has been delayed considerably. I mentioned in Chapter 2 that these evil twins are two of the Eight Great Barriers to reaching your retirement destination. Let me show you just how devastating the effects of inflation and income taxes can be.

Let's say you are going to retire at age sixty-five, which is twenty years away. Currently, your monthly requirement to live in a reasonably comfortable manner is $3,000, excluding the mortgage payment (we are assuming that the house has been paid off.) At an annual inflation rate of just 4 percent, this means that your living costs will inflate to over $6,573 per month at retirement. By the time you are seventy-five, these monthly costs could surpass $9,730! Sounds far-fetched and totally unrealistic, right? Wrong!

Yes, I know that some of your costs are not going to go up significantly—clothing, dining out, etc. will probably diminish as the years go by. But have you taken a look at the necessities, such as health care, food, and energy? These costs have been going up at a significantly higher rate than just 4 percent in the past few years. In fact, the Centers for Medicare and Medicaid Services (CMS) released a study in early 2003 stating that in 1990, we spent 12 percent of the gross domestic product (GDP) on healthcare. Today, it's at 14.8 percent, and is scheduled to rise to 17.8 percent by 2012.

In 2002, we spent $5,427 per person on healthcare, almost exactly double what we spent in 1990 (a 6 percent annual hike, based on the "Rule of 72"). CMS estimates that we will be spending $9,972 by 2012, and this does not even reflect the fact that more and more baby boomers will be getting older and needing medical care. There seems to be no end to the spiraling increases in the cost of these necessities.

To further prove the point, let's step back twenty years. At an annual inflation rate of 4 percent, items that cost $3,000 today could have been bought then for less than $1,370 then. Let's compare the cost of some items listed in **Exhibit 2-1**, which lists the **Average Annual Increase (in percent) from 1960-2005.**

	1960	1980	2005	Average Annual Increase (%) (1960-2005)
A Quart of Milk:	$0.26	$0.53	$1.29	3.62
A Loaf of White Bread:	$0.21	$0.51	$1.06	3.66
A Dozen Eggs:	$0.58	$0.85	$1.28	1.77
A Pound of Round Steak:	$1.06	$2.77	$3.94	2.96
A Postage Stamp:	$0.04	$0.13	$0.37	5.07

If you were to look at just the annual rate of inflation of these items over the past forty-five years, you wouldn't give it a second thought. After all, we can certainly handle inflation as tame as 5.07 percent, as in the case of the cost of mailing a first-class letter. But look what that "benign" rate of interest—just 5.07 percent—did to the cost in forty-five years: it went up more than nine-fold, and in 2006, it went up to $0.39! Using the "Rule of 72" at a rate of 5.07 percent, we see that the cost of a first-class postage stamp will double again in less than fourteen years. No wonder e-mail is so popular!

In my approach to planning for client retirements, I always stress the utilization of "conservative assumptions." Inflation may not be a big threat in the future—perhaps it could be as little as 1 percent. But can you really afford to take that chance? No, not really. You have to make allowances for that great barrier to your Golden Pond.

The case of the cheapening dollar

Debt is the only area of your personal finances that may not be affected by inflation. For example, if you have a commitment to pay a certain amount every month over the life of your fifteen- or thirty-year mortgage, the monthly payments for principal and interest will remain the same or decrease if you refinance (unless, of course, you move into a higher-priced home with a higher mortgage).

The fact remains, though, that you will be paying off that mortgage with "cheaper dollars" in the future, thanks to inflation. A similar conclusion can be reached in the case of life insurance and long-term disability payments, which will remain constant during the period you are covered. Like the mortgage, you will be making those payments with "cheaper dollars" in the future. Of course, the proceeds from the life insurance policy may also be worth a lot less than today's face value, but that's what inflation does to the value of the dollar. Ditto if you should happen to win the Lotto!

For example, let's say you have a thirty-year level premium term insurance coverage for $1 million, and your premium is $1,000 per year. By the last year of your coverage, the "real" value of your payment (in terms of today's dollars) could be approximately $300, thanks to an annual inflation rate of 4 percent (hopefully it will also represent a decreasing percentage of your total income). However, just as inflation helps you in that regard, it can hurt you in another. The $1 million your beneficiaries would receive if you were to die in the thirtieth year of your coverage could only be worth approximately $300,000 in terms of today's dollars! **Exhibit 2-5** shows the declining value of the dollar. According to government statistics, a dollar in 1967 was worth only seventeen cents in 2005. Truly astounding, isn't it?

Now, to get an idea of what it would take to get to Golden Pond, review the Retirement Living Expenses Worksheet (**Exhibit 3-4**) you completed in Chapter 3. Keep in mind that some of these expenses could go on increasing due to inflation even after you have reached Golden Pond. It will take some planning and management of your resources to ensure that you can continue to live on Golden Pond.

Income Taxes

There are only two things certain in life: death and taxes. *If you are dead, the problem is solved*. You will never have to pay income taxes again. But you have to admit, that's a pretty steep price to pay for tax avoidance. So, you have to learn to live with it.

Through proper planning, you can try to minimize the impact of taxes so that more money flows into your pockets rather than the government's. If you don't familiarize yourself with some of the finer details, life could become a living death. Your Golden Pond could be drained so much it starts to resemble the dry creek we've been trying to avoid all along.

Exhibit 5-1 shows the income tax rates for the year 2006. Keep in mind that these are just federal income taxes. To this amount, you have to add the state and local income taxes, as well as social security and Medicare withholding. When you consider that at some income levels, a taxpayer begins to get phased out of exemptions and deductions and can even be subjected to the dreaded Alternative Minimum Tax, it is entirely possible that the maximum marginal income tax bracket for some taxpayers could easily surpass 50 percent. That means, **depending on where you live and the money you make, more than half of every additional dollar you earn goes toward the payment of taxes.**

It is, therefore, imperative that you learn to understand the impact of taxes on your ability to save and invest for the future. (See **Exhibit 2-6** in case you need to see the impact of taxes once again.) For example, you may be planning to withdraw a certain amount from your IRA at retirement. Granted, withdrawals from IRAs are not subject to social security and Medicare withholding, and in some lucky states they aren't even subject to state income taxes. But you **would** have to allow for federal income taxes when determining how much to withdraw. If you need $30,000 to live on, the withdrawal would have to be, say, $35,000 with perhaps $5,000 being used to pay the federal income taxes (note: this is only an example to make the point!).

Let's look at an annual $1,000 investment with two different scenarios (a total of $25,000 invested over twenty-five years): one in a tax-deferred account, and one in an account that is subject to tax that has a compounded annual rate of return of 10 percent at a **marginal** (i.e. not average) income tax rate of 30 percent. To reinforce the point of **Exhibit 2-6,** let us take a look at **Exhibit 5-2.** This exhibit shows you the difference between tax-deferred and annual taxation of your investment account. As you can see, that difference gets more and more substantial as the years go by. This is why investing in IRA's or in your company 401(k) plans is so popular. At the end of twenty-five years, the tax-deferred account is ahead by almost 95 percent—almost twice the amount of the taxable account! When you add to this the impact of state income taxes, the difference becomes even more glaring. *Hey, wait a minute*, you might say. *Don't you have to pay taxes on the money you have accumulated in the tax-deferred account somewhere along the line?* You are catching on fast. See, I told you that you would be more financially astute by the time you were done with this book. Yes, it is sad but true. You do have to pay taxes on that growth at a later date. Hopefully, it will be at a time when you are in a lower marginal tax bracket, but let's take a look and see the impact. Assuming that the tax rate stays the same, as most retirees often find out to their dismay, **Exhibit 5.2** shows that the difference in after-tax growth is almost 36 percent! In other words, tax-deferral netted you over 36 percent more than paying taxes as you go. Overall, considering your final balances, the exhibit shows the tax-deferred account as being ahead by 23 percent. This is after *intentionally* skewing the data by making *all* of the tax-deferred growth subject to tax at once. In reality, most individuals only withdraw amounts that they need for their yearly or monthly expenses, or as in the case of the IRS rules for people who are age seventy and a half, they are forced to withdraw a certain minimum amount based on life expectancy. You can use whichever percentage you want to in this example—36 percent or 23 percent. **The fact remains that the difference is substantial** Now do you understand why tax planning plays such an important role in your journey to Golden Pond?

One of the primary objectives in analyzing your income tax situation is to minimize the loss due to taxation and maximize the opportunity for accumulating personal wealth. Can an individual eliminate income taxes completely? It is possible at certain low levels of income. For the most part, though, if you have income, you will have to pay. The objective is not tax elimination as much as tax reduction or tax minimization.

There are several ways one can achieve this worthwhile goal. **Remember that every dollar you save by reducing your taxes can go to funding your Golden Pond**.

You can reduce the impact of income taxes by:

Tax Deferral: contributing as much as you are allowed into your IRAs, 401(k) plans, and even annuities. The 401(k)s are a wonderful mechanism. Not only do you NOT have to pay income taxes on the money you put into these plans, but, in most cases, the company might even match your contributions. In my opinion, people who do not participate in this plan when their employers offer it are missing one of the best ways of savings for their Golden Pond.

Income Shifting: shifting income to your children, who have a lower marginal tax rate than you. For example, children typically do not pay any taxes on the first $700 of investment income and may pay as little as 10 percent on the next $700, for an average of 5 percent on the first $1,400. If your tax bracket is 30 percent, that's a saving of 25 percent, or $350. If you have a small business, you might be able to shift some income to family members who are employees of the business, thus shifting some of your higher-taxed income to your lower-taxed children. There are other, more sophisticated techniques for shifting income, but those are beyond the scope of this book.

Repositioning Assets: You can do this by moving into tax-free investments or reducing your exposure to investments that produce current income (interest, dividends) that you really do not need in order to maintain your current lifestyle.

Utilizing Favorable Rules: this entails selling appreciated real estate in a like-kind exchange program, utilizing the installment method on the sale of an asset, utilizing the homeowner's exclusion on the sale of the primary residence, and even utilizing the step-up of cost basis on appreciated assets that have been bequeathed to you. You can also "bunch up" your itemized tax deductions by planning to pay all of your deductible expenses to the extent possible in a particular year to meet the threshold requirements for medical expenses (7.5 percent of Adjusted Gross Income) or miscellaneous expenses (2 percent of Adjusted Gross Income). The "bunching" strategy is very useful in cases where one does not have enough deductions to itemize them in a particular year, but by paying some of the expenses that qualify for deductibility from the following year, the tax payer would qualify for and benefit from the itemization of deductions. Prepayment of personal property taxes and state-estimated income taxes are also popular ways of bunching your deductions.

Now that we know what inflation and taxes can do to your nest egg, let's take a look at the impact that inflation and income taxes can have on your investments.

Example:

1. What is your pre-Tax Rate of Return?	<u>8.0</u> %
2. What is your Marginal Income Tax Bracket? (i.e., the rate at which each additional dollar of income is taxed)	<u>30.0</u> %
3. Percentage Left After Taxes? (100 percent – Line 2)	<u>70.0</u> %
4. After-Tax Rate of Return? (Line 1 X Line 3)	<u>5.6</u> %
5. Assumed Inflation Rate for the year?	<u>3.0</u> %
6. Rate of Return Adjusted for Inflation and Taxes?	<u>2.6</u> %

In the example above, you can see how an inflation rate of *just* 3.0 percent and a marginal income tax bracket of 30 percent can reduce an 8.0 percent return to 2.6 percent. Utilizing the "Rule of 72", it would take only nine years to double your money at 8 percent, but it would take almost twenty-seven years at 2.6 percent. And that, ladies and gentlemen, is the true impact of inflation and taxes. Ignore these facts at your own peril.

Exhibit 5-1

Individual Tax Rate Schedules		
Filing Status	**Rate (%)**	**Income Tax Rate Schedules for 2006***
Single		
	10	**0 – 7,550**
	15	**6,551 – 30,650**
	25	**30,651–74,200**
	28	**74,201 – 154,800**
	33	**154,801 – 336,550**
	35	**Over 336,550**
Head of Household		
	10	**0 – 10,750**
	15	**10,751 – 41,050**
	25	**41,051 – 106,000**
	28	**106,001 – 171,650**
	33	**171,651 – 336,550**
	35	**Over 336,550**
Married Filling Jointly (And Surviving Spouses)		
	10	**0 – 15,100**
	15	**15,101 – 61,300**
	25	**61,301 – 123,700**
	28	**123,701 – 188,450**
	33	**188,451 – 336,550**
	35	**Over 336,550**
Married Filling Separately		
	10	**0 – 7,550**
	15	**7,551 – 30,650**
	25	**30,651 – 61,850**
	28	**61,851 – 94,225**
	33	**94,226 – 168,275**
	35	**Over 168,275**

(*)These bracket amounts are the estimated tax brackets for 2006. As we go to press, the IRS has not announced the official 2006 inflation adjustments.

Exhibit 5-2
Difference between Tax-Deferred and Taxable Growth

(Assume an annual investment of $1,000 at an annual rate of return of 10 percent over twenty-five years, 30 percent tax bracket)

No. of Years	Tax Deferred Account			Taxable Account			Difference	
	Balance	Amount Invested	Growth	Balance	Amount Invested	Growth	(C) – (F)	
	(A)	(B)	(C)	(D)	(E)	(F)	Amount	Percentage
5	6,716	5,000	1,716	6,153	5,000	1,153	563	49
10	17,531	10,000	7,531	14,784	10,000	4,784	2,747	57
15	34,950	15,000	19,950	26,888	15,000	11,888	8,062	68
20	63,002	20,000	43,002	43,865	20,000	23,865	19,137	80
25	108,182	25,000	83,182	67,676	25,000	42,676	40,506	95
Tax at 30 percent on Growth after twenty-five years		24,940			0			
Net Growth		58,242			42,676		15,566	36
Balance after twenty-five years, after taxation		83,242			67,676		15,566	23

Chapter 6

Risk Management

NOW THAT YOU'VE finished assessing where you are and where you want to be at retirement, it's time to figure out some of the curves life can throw at you and how vulnerable you are to those curves. These vulnerabilities have the potential of destroying whatever plans you may have developed for your future. If you fail to address them instead of being On Golden Pond, you will really be Up the Creek!

Just to give you an idea of what I am talking about… what good is it to save a certain amount of money per month towards your retirement if you are not properly covered for, say, auto insurance? One accident (sometimes it doesn't even have to be your fault!) could result in the loss your entire savings nest egg, which you have worked so diligently to build.

The area of personal finance where you determine your vulnerabilities and the actions you need to take to reduce or eliminate them is called risk management. In reality, the solutions to risk management involve the purchase of insurance to offset the losses that have the potential of financially wiping out you and your family. On occasion, you may decide that you are willing to take the chance of a financial loss, either because the premium is too high or because the chances of such an occurrence are very remote. In such cases, you are considered to be "self-insured." In most cases, self-insurance is not a good idea and for some particular coverage (e.g. auto), the state authorities may force you to have the proper insurance.

No one likes talking about insurance, and they like to meet or talk with an insurance agent even less. Perhaps because of the complexities involved in trying to compare various alternatives in a meaningful way, I have found that there is a tremendous amount of distrust of insurance and of the person who is recommending it. This is the root cause of people being under-insured. The suspicion of insurance agents, the complexity involved in comparing alternatives, and yes, the cost itself, paralyzes people to the point where a person takes no action to remove the vulnerability even though he realizes that he absolutely needs to do something. He is afraid of being "taken," or he is afraid of coming across as an idiot for asking what may turn out to be a simple question. Most of the time, he doesn't even know what questions to ask. This is unfortunate because insurance plays a vital role in your ability to reach Golden Pond. After all, who wants to think about their sudden death or a disability that could knock them out of the work force for the rest of their lives? No one wants to think of being sued, losing his job, or being hit by an uninsured driver who may or may not be driving under the influence. A catastrophic illness or an extended hospital stay? Perish the thought! But this reluctance to deal with the "darker side of life" is exactly why so many thousands of people see their dreams go up in smoke when a single disaster hits.

Folks, you have to tackle your insurance just as you would tackle stocks, bonds, or real estate investments. You want to invest in something that will provide a safety net for your future. Believe me, there's no better safety net than insurance. **Ignoring the matter because you don't like insurance, or because you don't like an insurance agent, or any other reason you use to justify your decision is tantamount to playing Russian roulette with your financial security**. If you ignore this part of your financial picture just because you don't understand it or don't trust the salesman, you could hurt your own chances of getting to Golden Pond.

The biggest mistake people make about insurance.

When it comes to insurance, most people make the mistake of not getting enough coverage. They are guilty of under-coverage in a specific type of insurance (i.e. life, disability, long-term care, medical, auto, home). On occasion, they may decide to self-insure for a certain category of coverage; for example, a lot of people may decide (for whatever reason) that it is not worth the annual premium to protect themselves from nursing home costs by getting long-term care insurance, figuring they will pay the costs of their nursing home stay from their own pockets if and when such an eventuality occurs. They may also decide to do the same with other types of insurance.

It is one thing to be under-insured or to just have enough insurance to get by, and perhaps even not get some particular type of insurance because you cannot afford it. It is a totally different matter if you can afford insurance, but are unwilling to spend the money required for the premiums.

I have found that most people take the latter course of action because they do not fully realize the financial ramifications of their choices, or, again, because they don't trust insurance agents. They figure that premiums are "money down the drain" because if they don't make any claims, they lose the money. In a sense, they are rolling the dice and hoping that luck will favor them. When you are considering your vulnerabilities and wondering whether to get the various forms of insurance, and in what amount, be prepared to consider the other side of the equation: **what happens if things go wrong?** How will that affect you and your family's ability to reach Golden Pond, your retirement nirvana?

In this chapter, I will review some of the principal financial vulnerabilities and the appropriate insurance policies pertaining to them. They are: premature death, long-term disability, catastrophic illness, auto accident (which can result in significant personal and property damage), and even death insurance. There is a potential for lawsuits against you as a homeowner, an auto owner, a professional, an employer, or in any other role you see yourself playing as you make your way through life.

The solution to reducing or eliminating these vulnerabilities is, of course, insurance of one form or another. As mentioned before, you may decide *not* to obtain coverage for a certain vulnerability.

That is totally acceptable **as long as the law allows you to do so, and more importantly, as long as you have considered the pros and cons of such a decision.**

Before we address the various types of insurance available to resolve these financial vulnerabilities, it is important to keep the following things in mind as you evaluate the various choices within each type of insurance.

1. Do your homework

Review the safety ratings of the companies you are evaluating. It is not entirely impossible for an insurance company to go under. Generally speaking, you should choose the one that's most financially sound—even if sometimes you may wind up paying a higher premium. You do not want to choose the cheapest policy, only to have the insurer go under a few years later. This would create inconvenience and extra work for you at the very least, and, on occasion, you may lose the coverage completely because you have become uninsurable during the time you had the prior coverage.

2. Choose the variables carefully.

Options are those items (the "bells and whistles") within a policy that could impact your benefits and/or the premiums you pay. A deductible on your auto or medical policy is the amount you are liable for before the insurance kicks in. The higher the deductible, the lower the premium. In a way, the deductible can be considered part of one's "self-insurance." The elimination, or waiting period, for a disability or long-term care policy would be the amount of time the policy holder is willing to wait and spend his own money before the insurance coverage begins. Possible waiting periods could be zero days, thirty days, ninety days, etc. Again, the longer the waiting period, the lower the premium. Once more, this option can be considered part of one's decision to self-insure. The mode of premium payment (annually, semi-annually, quarterly, monthly) could also impact the premium, with the annual mode being the least expensive, and the monthly mode being the most expensive due to a certain amount of interest and administrative charge that is levied over and above the annual premium. A typical charge might be 2 percent over and above the annual amount for the semi-annual mode, 4 percent for the quarterly mode, and as much as 8.5 percent for the monthly mode of premium payment. Most insurance companies also want the right to take the money out of your checking account automatically ("checkomatic") if you opt for the monthly mode. This may or may not be to your liking and is something you should consider.

Keep in mind that these various options (the "bells and whistles") can add up very quickly, and what appears to be affordable coverage could quickly turn into an exorbitant amount. In this regard, **it is essential that you learn to differentiate between the "must have" and the "nice to have" options.**

3. Review your coverage periodically (annually, preferably)

The objective of the review is to ensure that your current vulnerabilities are addressed by the coverage you have. I recently came across a professional banker who had not changed the limits on her auto insurance coverage in over thirty years! She was lucky that she was never involved in an accident or a claim, which could have devastated her financially, jeopardizing her present and her future. I can't tell you how many horrible stories I hear from people who thought they were well protected until a certain tragic event occurs that makes them realize the awful truth: they were not covered or protected as well or as much as they had thought.

Now let us talk about the various types of insurance to help you eliminate or reduce the vulnerabilities we talked about earlier. Remember, the purpose here is not to provide you with the *definitions* of these types of insurance; you can get that anywhere. Rather, I am here to point out how some of these options could help reduce your vulnerabilities, which will help you get to Golden Pond that much faster.

Life Insurance

Life Insurance has the great benefit of protection against the sudden and untimely death of the breadwinner of the family. It has other advantages, too, including protection against loss resulting from the death of a key employee, providing an estate to pay estate taxes that could potentially take away more than half of the estate of a descendent, etc. However, since we are still trying to get to Golden Pond, it is the vulnerability of the breadwinner (the key person, such as the spouse), whose premature death could devastate a family's plans, that I am addressing here.

What happens to the surviving spouse and children if the breadwinner of the family were to die prematurely? Would the surviving spouse be able to pay the mortgage, college expenses, etc. in addition to the daily living expenses? Would he or she be forced to go to work to make ends meet? Life insurance serves these needs. It provides financial protection for the survivors, and therefore, it is extremely critical that adequate life insurance be part of the foundation of your financial security. Of course, there are exceptions to that rule; if your circumstances are such that no one would be financially affected by your premature death, you may decide that you do not need this coverage. But if you are young, married parents, and you don't have enough net worth, it is absolutely imperative that you get this coverage. In fact, eliminating this vulnerability might be the highest priority under such circumstances.

Adequate life insurance is important. However, exactly what qualifies as adequate? Many people buy insurance in "round numbers": 100,000, 250,000, 500,000, 1,000,000, etc. That, in and of itself, is not bad. But most people have not done any homework to determine whether or not that "round number" will be enough. There are many different ways to determine just how much life insurance you need. **Exhibit 6-1** is one such example. Once you determine what you need, you can then round up to a *higher* number. For example, if you determine that an adequate amount is $227,000, then you can round up to $250,000, but you definitely cannot round down to $200,000 unless cost becomes a consideration.

Another key issue is deciding which color and flavor best suits you. The most common forms of life insurance are: term life, whole life, universal life, and variable life Again, let me remind you: This is *not* a book on life insurance. As such, I am not going to go into details on each specific type of insurance. You can get that information in any insurance book or even online. The main thing to keep in mind is that term insurance is the cheapest type of insurance. The premium will not change for a specified number of years for term insurance, unless it happens to be "annual renewable term insurance" (ART), where the insurance premiums starts off very low and then rises every year until it reaches preposterous levels. While there may be a use for ART insurance in some unique situations, it is the "level premium" term insurance that I am recommending in this book. No matter what type of term insurance you get, keep in mind that there is no build up of cash value in this type of policy. That is, when the policy matures or lapses, you do not get anything back from the premiums you paid over the years. As such, you cannot borrow from the cash value of this policy because there is no cash value.

In most cases, though, the difference in annual premiums between term coverage and the other three types (cash value) coverage is so great that it almost behooves a young family starting out to obtain the maximum amount of coverage based on the premiums they can afford to pay. Term insurance fits the bill in this regard, and it offers the biggest bang for your buck. Moreover, based on the premiums you are willing to pay, term insurance policy premiums remain constant over ten, fifteen, twenty, and, for some, even thirty years!

A young man in his early thirties could get term life insurance coverage of one million dollars, for example, at an annual premium of less than a thousand dollars! And the premium would be even lower for a woman with the same coverage. Moreover, the premium would not change for as long as thirty years if he so desired. The annual premiums would be even lower if the coverage was needed for a lesser period. Due to the time value of money (a thousand dollars might only be worth seven hundred, for example, when inflation is considered), and the fact that your income is expected to rise in the future, the life insurance premium takes up less and less of your annual income as the years go by. Of course, the million dollar coverage would also be worth less as the years go by, and that is why you need to make sure that your coverage is adequate.

There is one other type of term life coverage where the premium goes up every year, called "annual renewable term." This coverage can start off very inexpensive, but it gets to be downright exorbitant and almost unaffordable after several years. It does have the advantage of providing you with coverage forever, as long as you keep paying the premiums, which is unlike the ten-, fifteen-, twenty-, or thirty-year level premium policies that mature eventually. In most cases, I do not recommend this type of life insurance.

Because term insurance is so much cheaper than other types of life insurance, proponents of term life often use the expression, *buy term, invest the difference.* In other words, the extra money you save by not purchasing other types of policies could be used to invest and build up your own cash value instead of having the insurance company do it for you. I, too, am a firm believer in that concept. I just do not believe in paying the insurance company fees to manage my money for me. I know myself and much better than the insurance company ever could, and I like to have control over my investments.

The other three types of life insurance offer more permanent types of coverage. They not only provide cash value, but they are also guaranteed renewable as long as the premium payments are made. And, of course, they offer the ability to borrow against the cash value in the policy. These loans can provide money to you down the road to help with temporary needs or emergencies at extremely reasonable interest rates. Some people use these types of permanent insurance to fund their retirement, their children's college educations, etc. or for other special situations where life term insurance would not be practical. Again, I plead guilty to being biased, but, in my opinion, term life insurance offers the best value for a young family or for someone on a tight budget. Unfortunately, there is no one answer as to which type of insurance is the best. The real answer depends on your needs and circumstances. How do you decide which type of life insurance works best for you? Look for a policy with benefits and premiums that most closely match your present and future needs, as well as your ability to pay. Working with an insurance professional can help you decide which type of coverage is best suited for your needs. The professional can also help you determine HOW MUCH insurance you need. Most people usually select a nice, round number, such as $100,000, or $250,000, or $500,000, or even $1 million and more. However, if you are on a budget, you want to make sure that you buy only what you feel is necessary, and use the extra money in your budget for other priorities. The worksheet mentioned previously (**Exhibit 6-1**) can help provide you with at least a rough idea of what your needs are.

Long-Term Disability

If you had a machine that was capable of printing dollar bills worth $50,000 a year, what would you insure it for? Most people would say $50,000. Yet most of these same people probably do not have any disability insurance. In reality, your body is like that machine that can produce $50,000 per year. So how is it that you do not want to insure it to make sure that it continues to do so? People fail to consider what would happen if they had an accident or illness that prevented them from producing that income. How would they replace that income? How would they meet all of their financial obligations? If you don't think it can happen to you, think again. I have read statistics in several publications which report that a person in his thirties or forties is about three to five times more likely to be disabled than die. While I am positive about the likelihood, I have never seen the actual number substantiated anywhere. Regardless of that, the fact remains that ignoring this vulnerability on the mistaken premise that it cannot happen to you is extremely foolish and potentially dangerous. While your savings is imperative for short-term emergencies, it's certainly not meant to be used for long-term issues. Once your savings is gone, it's gone! Borrowing money when you're disabled is almost an impossibility, too, as you usually need proof of income to obtain a loan. Even social security refuses to kick in unless the disability is expected to last at least twelve months or result in death. Moreover, you must be so severely impaired, physically or mentally, **that you cannot perform any substantial gainful work!**

It's best to make plans now for income replacement. Disability insurance helps you meet your ongoing financial responsibilities by paying you a monthly income when you're sick, hurt, or otherwise unable to work. When choosing your disability policy, you'll be asked to consider the following variables, which will affect the cost:

1. The amount of coverage you need monthly.

Keep in mind that the maximum coverage you can get is limited to a certain percentage of your current income (say, approximately two-thirds or 67 percent). So, if your current income is $60,000 per year, you might be limited to a maximum coverage of $40,000. You cannot get paid the full amount of $60,000 by insuring yourself with two companies for $30,000 each, and you certainly cannot get paid in disability more than your income by insuring yourself with multiple companies to obtain coverage for, say, $75,000. **An important thing to keep in mind: if your employer has been paying the premiums, or if you have been paying the premiums with before-tax dollars, the payments you receive for long-term disability will be subject to income taxation.** Let us say that your average tax rate is 15 percent. The $40,000 you received in the previous example would be reduced to $34,000 after tax. That's almost half of what you earned before your disability, and if your annual expenses are, say, $45,000, then you are truly "Up the Creek!"

So, PLEASE make sure that you are adequately covered for long-term disability. I have seen too many lives and too many marriages ruined due to the financial devastation caused by the breadwinner's disability.

2. How long you want benefits to be paid to you if you remain totally disabled.

The duration typically could be one year, five years, life, or until the age social security kicks in. Obviously, the longer the period of coverage, the higher the cost.

3. How long you must be disabled before your benefits kick in, otherwise referred to as the "waiting" or "elimination period."

The longer the waiting period, the lower the cost. A policy with a one year waiting period is considerably less expensive than one offering a waiting period of, say, thirty days. But if you were disabled, would you have the financial resources to survive a year before those benefits kicked in?

4. Cost of Living Adjustments

If you want your disability benefits to be adjusted for inflation, it will cost you more than if you don't. Plus, you will have to decide between "simple interest" and "compound interest" for the calculation. I showed you the difference between the two in Chapter 2, and hopefully, you learned enough to figure out that benefits with compound rates are greater. Obviously, the cost of the rider for compound interest would be higher than that for simple interest.

5. Integration with Social Security

You could choose to have your disability payments integrated with your social security payments for disability to lower the cost of the premium for coverage. This essentially means that the insurance company would reduce its disability payments to you by the amount you receive from Social Security. The insurance company pays less, so you pay less. It's as simple as that.

Medical/Health Insurance

These days, health insurance isn't an option, it's a necessity. Paying out of your pocket for medical expenses may work for an occasional prescription, but it's just not feasible when you're facing open-heart surgery. Health insurance offers protection against serious financial loss in case you're faced with a hospital stay or a disability. As I've noted before, hundreds of thousands of people experience catastrophic illness in some way before they reach retirement, but we are all exposed to the same risks. Without adequate health insurance, your pocket money and your savings can be gone in a flash. Again, remember that this is not a book on insurance. I am just outlining the areas you need to address if you want to be financially secure at a certain age. Therefore, we are not going to be discussing the intricate details of HMOs and PPOs and whether one type is better than the other.

The main objective is to ensure that your financial vulnerability to illness and catastrophic illness is addressed by the coverage you have or should have. This is definitely one area where you may want to think twice (and then think again) about being "self-insured," because **the possibility of losing your life savings as a result of a catastrophic illness is not that remote**.

We come across all types of horror stories in the news media—ones where a family has been ruined financially due to inadequate insurance or no insurance at all. This is the greatest country in the world. Even in health care, we are way ahead of every other country in terms of technology and care. Unfortunately, these items come at a horrific cost. If you have an illness that requires extended hospitalization or care and you are not properly insured, then no doubt about it, you will find yourself "Up The Creek." **The potential to get wiped out is real, and this huge vulnerability MUST to be addressed**.

Auto/Home Insurance

Again, we are addressing the need for coverage in these two areas to make sure that we do not get wiped out financially as a result of an accident involving our car or home. Auto insurance protects you against the financial risk associated with property damage and bodily injury caused by accidents (whether it's your fault or someone else's), vandalism, theft, or natural disasters (like a tree falling through your windshield). Home insurance protects you from financial loss by protecting your home and its contents against loss by fire, theft, storms, falling objects, objects that drive into your front window, and a host of other less-publicized tricks Mother Nature has a lot of tricks up her sleeve. Home insurance also covers personal liability (for instance, if someone were to be accidentally injured on your property) up to certain prescribed limits.

The basic auto insurance policy consists of liability coverage with limits established where you are protected for injuring someone up to certain previously-established limits for claims based on "per person," "per occurrence," and "property damage." So, if you have coverage of, say $100K/$300K/$50K, it means that the insurance company will pay each individual who has a claim against you for a specific occurrence (accident) up to $100,000 with a maximum payout of $300,000 per occurrence. Property damage would be limited to $50,000. If the claim against you exceeds these limits, you would be responsible for the excess. Some insurance companies do not have limits "per person" and instead only have limits per occurrence. In certain cases, a rider that is tacked on to your policy would protect you if you were caused bodily harm or property damage by an uninsured or an under-insured motorist. It is highly advisable to add such a rider on to your auto policy. As with all types of insurance, you have to make sure that you review your coverage periodically, assess its adequacy, and take appropriate and timely action, if needed.

Details such as collision coverage, comprehensive coverage, emergency roadside assistance, and rental car coverage can easily be answered by your property and casualty insurance agent. For some reason, people trust their property and casualty person a lot more than their life insurance person. Perhaps because property and casualty insurance is a little easier to understand, or perhaps because this insurance does not have to be a life-long commitment.

As far as home insurance is concerned, you have to make sure that you are covered for the "replacement cost" of the home and not for what you originally paid for it. You could have bought the home a long time ago and made extensive improvements since then, but your coverage could be considerably less than the money you would need to replace the home in case of a catastrophe.

It is a good idea to insure your valuables (jewelry, art, antiques, etc) with a separate rider rather than use the policy's standard coverage for that purpose. Just because you rent or live in a condominium or an apartment instead of a single-frame house doesn't mean you're off the hook. As a renter, you can assume your landlord has insurance on the home, but you'll need coverage to protect your personal property and protect you in liability situations.

Personal Liability Umbrella Insurance

If you are ever held liable for an accident involving your home or car, and you have exceeded the limits of your home or auto coverage, you will be personally responsible for the excess. In the previous segment, we discussed coverage of $100,000/$300,000/ $50,000 for "per person/per occurrence/property damage." If the claim were, for example, for $1 million, you would be responsible for coming up with the difference between that amount and the limit that applies (per person or per occurrence). In this case, it could be either $700,000 or $900,000. Regardless of which amount applies, just where are you going to come up with that kind of money? Even if you did have the money, it could probably devastate your retirement plans.

The answer to that dilemma is umbrella insurance. When any limit of your home or auto policy coverage is exceeded, this policy steps in and saves the day. It is so affordable that sometimes you wonder why more people do not obtain it. The annual premium for obtaining a $1 million umbrella coverage could be approximately $250- $500, depending on your geographic region and circumstances. **This cost is reasonable enough and should not prevent anyone from obtaining this essential coverage.**

Your boat or your second home might cost a little more to cover, but still, it is very, very affordable. The best part, in most cases, is that the second million dollars of coverage costs half of the cost of the first million. So, you could probably obtain coverage of $2 million for an annual premium of $750 or so.

This is **an absolute necessity**. It ensures that you do not get financially wiped out due to a property and casualty claim against you. This is a must have for all families, in my opinion. Amazingly, this is also one of the most overlooked items in a person's risk management program. One of the main reasons for this may be that insurance companies do not promote it as much as they should, and insurance agents do not make enough on it to make it worth their while. **If you get nothing else from this book, understand the need for umbrella insurance and do something about it.**

Malpractice Insurance

Also called "errors and omissions insurance," this is a **must have** for professionals in occupations that are particularly vulnerable to lawsuits from people who believe they have been wronged by the professional's incompetence, negligence, etc. **In the litigious society we live in, it is almost mandatory to obtain this coverage**. This insurance is expensive, and sometimes, as in the case of some specialty physicians, exorbitant.

Because of the ever-escalating cost of this insurance and the fact that professionals cannot afford to be without it, the decision is mostly based on how much coverage to obtain, and how much you should "self-insure." As in the case of some specialty physicians (orthopedic, cardiac), failure to obtain this insurance may even result in the professional shutting down his practice.

Again, just to make sure your risk management program is comprehensive and takes into account your vulnerability from your profession, it is essential that this coverage be addressed and reviewed periodically—perhaps more so than any other coverage because of the rapidly-escalating premiums.

Long-Term Care Insurance

With the aging of this country's population, and the fact that life expectancy is sky-rocketing, it is not surprising that long-term care insurance is gaining in popularity. In the Chicago area, for example, the basic cost of nursing home stay is almost $200 per day. With the "extras" added in (diapers, drugs, etc), the average daily rate could easily reach $250! A year's stay in a nursing home could therefore reduce your nest egg by over $90,000! In four years' time, you could be poorer by almost $400,000 (allowing for inflation). It is a small wonder that this vulnerability concerns seniors the most. They know they want to be independent, and they do not want to be a burden to their children. They have therefore struggled through life and saved a certain amount for their golden years. A nursing home stay, especially an extended one, has the potential of making them totally destitute and dependent on their children, or worse yet, the government.

Long-term care insurance does provide coverage for people with prolonged illnesses, disability, or other chronic conditions that don't allow them to function independently, and this is not just restricted to nursing home expenses. It also covers respite care, assisted living facilities, home health care, and adult day care (also known as custodial care).

Unfortunately, long-term care doesn't come cheap. The alternative, however, is usually far more expensive. If you receive skilled nursing care in your home three times a week, your annual bill would likely top $40,000. Even simple visits from a home health aide twice weekly will run an average of $25,000 a year.

No one likes to think of life in a nursing home, but it's important to understand that after the age of sixty-five, insurance statistics show that you have a 71.8 percent chance of being housed in one before your death. Normally, more than one-third of all nursing home expenses are paid out-of-pocket by you and your family. Unbeknownst to most, Medicare does not normally pay for long-term care. In most cases, Medicare prefers to only address skilled care in approved nursing homes during brief convalescent periods; it doesn't pay for skilled or home health aide care in the home. Sadly, many people are being forced to rely on Medicaid, which pays for about 50 percent of one's stay in a nursing home. In order to qualify, however, you have to meet federal poverty guidelines for income and assets. In most cases today, people will begin spending out-of-pocket for a nursing home in order to ensure a better quality of life. They end up spending their entire savings in a matter of one year to five years and then are forced to rely on Medicaid (normally reducing their quality of living in the process) for the remainder of their lives.

In my opinion, this is the worst way to go. How could you spend your entire life building a savings and lifestyle and planning for your glorious retirement future only to see that entire cash storehouse dwindle to nothing in a matter of *months?* What's worse, if you're incapacitated and in a nursing home, the financial burden will fall on your children. Don't force your children into the only decision they can make—spending their own savings or put you on Medicaid. That's an ugly responsibility to bear.

Many financial advisors will tell you that long-term care insurance is optional, particularly if you're having difficulty making ends meet. I say if there's *any* way you can do it, even if it requires adjusting your lifestyle to cover that expense today, *do it*. While you can never predict whether you'll need long-term care or not, and while you can certainly expect the very best health for your retirement years, I think it's too big a risk to take.

Be sure you can afford it on a long-term basis. Now, because long-term care policies are more expensive, you must consider not only whether you can continue to pay the premiums now, but if you'll be able to continue paying them when they begin to rise. While some marketing entities will assure you that your premium is "level" and will never rise, they cannot legally guarantee this.

Remember that the silent monster—inflation—will always be at work in your life. That, combined with the soaring costs of health care and the possible new tax laws that work against you, could push your premium cost up substantially. Unless your long-term care policy provides for inflation, consider investing in an inflation-protection rider to avoid owning a policy whose benefit hasn't kept pace with the increasing cost of health care.

Buy it now, while you're still healthy. If you have existing health problems that are likely to result in long-term care (not minor health problems), you'll be turned down. The less evidence of pre-existing conditions you have, the better. Note, too, that the longer you wait, the more expensive the premium will be. If you purchase the policy at age sixty-five it will be at least three to four times higher than if you buy it at age fifty. So, there you have it. Life insurance, long-term disability insurance, health insurance, auto and homeowner's insurance, personal liability insurance (also called an umbrella policy), malpractice insurance, and long-term care insurance all play an important role in ensuring our financial well-being. They constitute your risk management program, and they need to be addressed based on your own individual circumstances. In the end, with all types of insurance, you will need to balance the benefits of being covered for any and all eventualities and the cost of such coverage, versus being covered for the minimum amount (or not at all) and low cost. The answer lies somewhere in between, where there is a good balance between cost and benefits. **Only you can determine what balance is good for you.** You can enlist the aid of a trusted professional, but in the end, the financial decision is up to you.

Okay, I've given you the basics. As I mentioned at the beginning of this chapter, it's up to you now to create your own safety net. And remember, your ability to reach and stay on Golden Pond is at stake here, so don't short-change yourself on the time and money needed to ensure your ultimate financial wellness and peace of mind.

Exhibit 6-1
Do You Really Need Any (or More) Life Insurance?

1. Estimated Annual Expenses of Survivors (spouse, children, etc.)

[Good estimate: 75 percent of current yearly expenses] $ _____

2. Less: Estimated Annual Income of Survivors

    A. Survivor Salary, If Any $ _____

    B. Social Security Benefits $ _____

    C. Pension Benefits $ _____

    D. Annuities or Other $ _____

    Total Estimated Annual Income of Survivors $ _____

3. Net Shortfall

[Line 1 minus Line 2] $ _____

[Note: If Line 2 exceeds Line 1, STOP. No additional life Insurance needed]

4. Amount of Money Required to Overcome Shortfall

[Line 3 divided by expected rate or return on your investments

e.g., $10,000 / 5% return = $200,000 _____% Expected Rate of Return] $ _____

5. Plus: One-Time Expenses

    A. Estate Taxes, If Any $ _____

    B. Mortgage Pay-off $ _____

    C. College Education Fund $ _____

    Total One-Time Expenses $ _____

6. Total Amount of Money Required (Line 4 + Line 5) $ _____

7. Less: Current Position

    A. Cash and Investments $ _____

    B. Life Insurance Coverage $ _____

    Total Current Position $ _____

8. Additional Life Insurance Required

[Line 6 minus Line 7. None required if Line 7 exceeds Line 6] $ _____

Chapter 7

Investing for Golden Pond: How NOT to Find Yourself Up the Creek at Retirement

SINCE I HAVE almost twenty-five years of experience dealing with stocks, bonds, and mutual funds, my observations and comments directly pertain to those types of investments. However, the same comments and observations could easily apply to other investments of your choice—real estate, commodities, small businesses, etc.

Of all of the items that have an impact on your ability to reach Golden Pond, investing is probably the most significant. This is the "engine" for the boat that is going to get you to Golden Pond. How you invest for your future, and the results of your investing strategy, can make or break you. In the late nineties, many people were enjoying returns of 25 percent or more on their stock market investments. It was hard to go wrong. Stories of investors doubling their money virtually overnight were found everywhere, and newsstands were overflowing with financial publications touting "The Ten Hottest Stocks To Buy Now!" Stock market "gurus" filled the airwaves, pontificating about the "new era" that we were in, and how the Dow Jones Industrial Average would quintuple, or at least quadruple, within ten years.

At any given time, fear or greed rules the markets, and at that particular time, greed was running rampant. People lost all sense of valuations and started chasing stocks (technology stocks in particular), hoping to get rich quick and sell the stocks to someone who would be dumb enough to pay even more than what they paid (in financial lingo, that's "the greater fool" theory).

If the price of tomatoes were to suddenly jump from $1 per pound to, say, $3 per pound, shoppers would find alternate foods to buy, right? It's logical and rational to do so. However, when it comes to stocks, the reaction is totally the opposite. If the price of a particular stock has jumped from $10 to $50 per share, investors will jump in with both feet and try to get as much as they can. Valuations, logic, and rationality are all left by the wayside in a mad scamper to get the over-priced stock.

Sure enough, in March 2000, the market turned around as the dot-com craze and technology industry hit the skids. Many people lost what they thought was the fortune they were going to use to retire. Some who had already retired were forced to go back to work, if they could even find jobs, while others moved to smaller, more affordable houses, leaving behind beautiful homes and precious memories. Some even filed for personal bankruptcy. In the end, many people found themselves Up The Creek!

"How could I have been so blind?" "Why didn't I take my profits?" "What was I thinking?" These were familiar laments from millions of people who learned the hard way that day trading, or chasing the hottest fund, was not the route to Golden Pond. Today, you'll hear so many of these very same individuals swear they will never let this happen to them again. They claim to have seen the light. They are now "born again" investors.

However, human nature being what it is, I am willing to bet that many of these same people will be back as soon as they see a bull market or the prospect for quick profits. People never seem to learn. I guess the desire to get rich quick is just too strong for them to ignore. In fact, even in the current stock market, we have begun to see a revival of the greed factor; this time, with stocks of companies in Southeast Asia, principally China and India. These people get bitten by the greed bug as they see their friends, relatives, or neighbors making money and dive right back into the very same situations that originally lost them so much of their money and put them so much further behind on their journey to Golden Pond. **Chasing returns and throwing caution to the winds is really no way to build a secure nest egg**. Those who do not learn from their mistakes are doomed to repeat them. And they do, over and over again.

After the stock market crash of 2000-2002, we saw the same mentality develop in real estate. People have been buying properties, sight unseen, in quite a few cases, with the hopes of "flipping" the investment for a quick profit. As interest rates continue to rise, it is a virtual certainty that some of these real estate "investors" will experience the same let-down that stock investors did from 2000-2002. And then people will move on to the next mania to create the next "bubble." Fear and greed are powerful human emotions, but neither has a place in responsible investing.

As I have been telling you all along, this is not going to be a chapter on the many different types of investment possibilities that are available, or the pros and cons of each one of them. Instead, this chapter is an exposé of the various pitfalls out there just waiting to capsize your boat and prevent you from reaching Golden Pond. It should be looked upon as an overall guide to investing wisely with the purpose of building toward your retirement goal. We will now look at the many ways in which people get steered off course and away from Golden Pond.

Specifically, we will look at some of the major pitfalls of investing (looking at *all* of the pitfalls would be a book by itself), and how to navigate your way around them. I will also pinpoint certain ideas and philosophies that have a major impact on your retirement security.

Common Pitfalls

There are so many mine fields to watch out for...so many boulders that can scuttle your boat. However, these are some of the most common reasons why some people just never make it to Golden Pond. Some of them look very similar to the Eight Great Barriers to Golden Pond, and in this chapter you will realize why.

1. Not having a written game plan.

As we mentioned in the introduction chapter of the book, if you don't know where you are going, any road will get you there! Folks, you have to know why you are investing, how you are going to invest, what you are going to invest in, when you are going to invest, when you want to get out (an exit strategy), where you will custody the accounts and execute the trades, how you are going to measure the performance (against your goals and/or benchmarks), etc. You need to know all of this **before you invest even a dime of your money.**

It is absolutely essential that you write down all of this (yes, you have to **write** it, not just think about it). This will be of tremendous help in preventing you from making decisions based purely on emotion (fear or greed). It would also help if you keep a scorecard on all of your investments, listing whether you made or lost money, how much and, more importantly, why you bought and sold. This will be of value not only at income-tax time, but also in avoiding past mistakes. I realize that this is time consuming and tedious, but if you are indeed serious about getting to your Golden Pond *and staying there,* it is truly worth the effort. Believe me, your investment discipline will help you get to your Golden Pond that much faster.

2. Falling prey to the greed bug

Okay, so your friend or neighbor mentions to you that he made a killing in a particular investment, be it a stock, real estate, or a commodity. Now you get bitten by the greed bug (I refer to this as "portfolio envy"), and you jump in with both feet. Soon enough, you may find yourself rapidly sinking. After you have lost a substantial portion of your investment, you swear never to do it ever again—that is, of course, until the next time such an "opportunity" comes along. I call this "The Ralph Kramden Syndrome" after the lovable loser character on the immortal show, "The Honeymooners." All you get for these various forays into the investment world is poorer, and further and further behind in your attempts to reach Golden Pond.

3. Falling prey to the fear bug

This is the exact opposite of the previously-mentioned greed bug. You have been told that "Uncle Louie" or a friend lost all of his hard-earned money in the stock market. Without trying to find out why or how or what amount that person claims to have lost, you decide that you are not going to invest in the stock market (or any type of investment, for that matter) or trust anyone with your money. As a result, you may feel you will not lose any money, but you will always be behind the curve in terms of investment performance, and your performance on an after-tax, after-inflation basis could suffer significantly (the result could even be negative!). In this scenario, you are basically going to take much longer to reach Golden Pond (if you reach it at all!). In a manner of speaking, you are basically fighting the current as you make your way upstream towards Golden Pond.

4. Lack of Proper Diversification / Improper Asset Allocation

It is a widely-accepted fact in financial circles that diversification helps you keep your level of risk under control. The basic theory of not putting all of your eggs in one basket is what asset allocation is all about. Keep in mind, though, that asset allocation by itself does not guarantee that you will not lose money. Proper allocation, though, will keep your fluctuations (volatility) under control. Proper allocation may not allow you to hit "home runs," but more importantly, it will considerably reduce your chances of "striking out." Keep in mind that if your investments decline from $1000 to $800, that's a 20 percent drop, and it requires a 25 percent gain just to get back to the original $1,000. Similarly, a 50 percent decline from $1,000 to $500 requires you to double your money just to get back your original investment. Hopefully, you can now see why it is so critical to keep those declines under control.

In my experience as an investment advisor, I have come across various people who decided to risk it all by putting all of their money in one stock or one investment. They could make huge amounts of money, but in almost every case, they have lost it all. They have swung for the fences and struck out. As a result, their retirement has been put in jeopardy, and if they were retired, most of them have had to return to work. Or, if they were already working, they find that they will have to continue working a lot longer than they had anticipated.

Proper asset allocation also means you have to diversify across various asset classes to minimize risk. **Just because you decide to buy ten different stocks or mutual funds does not mean you have diversified your risk**, at least not until you have figured out what asset class these securities belong to. The security could be large-cap, small-cap, international, emerging markets, etc. "Cap" is an abbreviation for capitalization, and it is calculated by multiplying the price per share of a stock by the number of its shares that are outstanding. You can see why Microsoft would be a large-cap stock. Similarly, bonds might belong to asset classes such as government, corporate, long-term, intermediate-term, or short-term. Some other asset classes may involve real estate, precious metals, emerging markets, etc. **Above all, just because you have invested your money with two or three different brokerages does not mean that you have diversified**. During the heyday of the Internet bubble, I remember reading a newspaper article where the reporter had talked to an investor about allocation. The investor mentioned that the only diversification that he needed was the four hot technology stocks that he was then invested in. I wonder how that investor feels today. Based on the names of the stocks he held at the time (Intel, Cisco, EMC, and Oracle), he could very easily have lost 80 percent or more of his investment.

The various asset classes that you decide to use in the composition of your portfolio must have as little correlation as possible between each other. The intent of diversification and proper allocation among various asset classes is that these asset classes have as low correlation between themselves as possible. The low correlation ensures that not all of the asset classes go up or down in tandem, and that if some go down, you have others in the portfolio that go up; thus, you cut down on the fluctuations, i.e. the risk or volatility.

This means that you have to plan your investment strategy and prepare to invest in various types of different investment vehicles to meet specific needs and risk profile. For example, you will typically look at stocks for growth and bonds for income. Then you will decide how much to allocate into each asset class listed in the previous paragraph based in part on your investment goals, in part on the economic climate and in part on how much of a risk you are comfortable taking. That allocation strategy should come way before diving into specific investments. A conservative investor might want to keep 55-60 percent in stocks for growth and 40-45 percent in bonds for income. Those broad categories would then be allocated among the respective components. For example, the stock portion may be split among large-cap growth, large-cap value, small-cap growth, small-cap value, emerging markets, international, real estate, and commodities, while the fixed income allocation could be split among treasury bonds, corporate bonds, international bonds, short-term bonds, intermediate-term bonds, and long-term bonds.

Someone on the verge of retiring and looking for retirement income might need such an allocation plan to generate the income necessary after retiring. Conversely, someone with many years before retirement, who is able to sleep at nights with a riskier portfolio, might look for more growth with, say, 80 percent growth and 20 percent income. Or they might look in growth alone, depending on age and risk-tolerance.

Asset allocation was highly unappreciated during the late nineties and the roaring bull market. People whose circumstances dictated otherwise wanted to put everything into technology stocks–100 percent of the money they had saved or could borrow. By the end of 2002, they had probably lost all of their gains and perhaps even their principal. They swore never to get into stocks and for safety they moved to bonds. Due to the falling interest rates, bonds did extremely well until rates started rising again in late 2005, and they found that perhaps bonds were not completely safe either. We are currently in a period of rising interest rates, and putting all of your money in bonds, especially long-term bonds (over five years) may make you just as vulnerable as having all of your money in small-cap stocks.

Since 2003, the stock market has been in a period of recovery, and these so-called investors have started chasing stocks once again. It's déjà vu, all over again, right? The fact is, all asset classes go through cycles when they are in favor and out of favor, and trying to guess when that is going to happen is an exercise in futility, as well as a quick way to lose money. A good asset allocation strategy takes care of that problem.

In addition to initially focusing on asset allocation, the wise investor will alter his or her strategy as necessary over time, in conjunction with retirement goals and changes that occur in life and in the markets. **Remember, investing is about making money and reaching financial security; it is not about keeping up with the Joneses.**

If you hire a professional, he may perform what is known as "Monte Carlo Simulation" on your asset allocation program. No, this has nothing to do with gambling, in spite of the name. This is just a powerful analytical tool allows you to determine the probability of achieving your stated goals with the particular allocation that you may have decided on. If you want higher (or lower) probability than what the analysis shows, you can tweak the allocations to better coincide with your risk tolerance and objectives. You can then perform Monte Carlo Simulation periodically to determine if your chances of achieving your retirement objectives have increased or decreased and then take appropriate action. In my opinion, Monte Carlo Simulation is an extremely useful tool that prevents you from making hasty decisions in the heat of the moment and truly enables you to stick to your investment game plan. Unfortunately, Monte Carlo Simulation is not that widely used by financial advisors and is virtually unheard of among lay people.

While no game plan is foolproof and no one sticks to their plan 100 percent of the time, the prudent investor thinks about goals and plans before looking to fill in the blanks with the specific investments. **Smart investing means sticking to a planned allocation of assets.** Believe me, it takes a tremendous amount of intestinal fortitude to stick to your chosen path.

From my own experience, I have found that retirees are more willing to stick to their asset allocation plans than younger investors. This is probably due to the fact that they realize they cannot afford to make a mistake and are willing to give up on the additional "juice" they may get from a hot category in exchange for peace of mind and retirement security. Generally, the older the person, the higher the likelihood he has of sticking to a "game plan." Younger people are much too quick to pull the trigger and go chasing after performance. They feel that they can always make up for it later. Unfortunately, it can take a long time to get out of the hole you dig for yourself. To reinforce what I mentioned at the beginning of this section, if you have lost 50 percent of your money (say, from $10,000 to $5,000), it will require you to make 100 percent on what's left. In other words, **you will need to double your money just to break even!**

5. Gambling with your money

What tends to happen very often is that people put the cart before the horse, or in this case, they focus on a specific investment before planning their investment strategy. Far too many investors chase the hot tip, be it a stock, a mutual fund, or another "get-rich-quick scheme." **When you are chasing returns like that, you are not investing; you are gambling**. If so, you are probably better off going to Las Vegas. At least you will have "fun" as you lose your nest egg. Sure your friend or neighbor may have made a million dollars on a stock. That doesn't mean you will. In fact, it is more likely that that ship has sailed and you're left holding the anchor as it falls into the water. A perfect example of this was in the late nineties when the market was going strong. People kept picking up the latest magazines and finding the "hot mutual funds to watch" and the "top funds for the coming year." How many really came through the following year? Perhaps 50 percent at best? Therefore, you were taking a 50-50 chance on the latest hot pick. This was no different than going to Las Vegas to play roulette and put all your money on red or black. Yes, you could double your money, but you could also go broke. **Can you really afford to take that chance with your retirement security?** I think not.

6. Misunderstanding risk:

In the world of investing, risk could be defined as the potential for losing money on your investment; sometimes, in fact, all of it. Just what kind of a risk are you willing to take to achieve your desired goals and objectives?

Too often people are swayed by the potential for growth and they are either not aware of, don't understand, or simply don't want to focus on the fact that the potential for a high returns also means there is a potential for greater losses. The possibility of a 50 percent or 100 percent gain drew tremendous amounts of people into high-risk mutual funds in the late nineties. What these people failed to realize was that if the bottom fell out and the market took a serious downturn (which it did), then they stood a chance of not only failing to make their big profit, but also of losing half or even all of the money they invested. When this happened to many people they were in shock. "How could I have lost so much?" was the question uppermost on their minds. Many investors failed to realize that this wasn't a break-even proposition, and that the worst-case scenario was not that they'd simply break even and get their initial investment back.

More conservative investing, which means taking less risk, isn't nearly as exciting and doesn't make for financial magazine headlines or interesting talk at dinner parties. If you put your money into an investment where you could lose 5 percent of your initial investment or make a 10 percent profit, people won't be lining up to hear your strategy. But the potential for 50 percent returns draws interest and people want to get onboard. The financial companies, however, don't like to add that there is also a potential for loss of 25 percent or 50 percent. You need to be aware of this when taking on higher risk investments. You also need to determine that you: A.) feel comfortable taking on such risk, and B.) can afford to lose a certain amount of money without destroying your overall financial plan (a trip to Las Vegas falls into this category for some people).

Volatility is another investing term that many people don't understand. It is essentially a term that quantifies risk. The fluctuation you can expect from an investment as in the examples mentioned above would be its volatility. Therefore, an investment with a potential return of -5 percent to +10 percent is less volatile, and therefore less risky than an investment with a potential return of -20 percent or +30 percent. Unfortunately, greed causes too many people to go after the +30 percent without looking at the other side of the range.

Historically speaking, stocks typically have a higher rate of return than government bonds—the greater the pain (volatility, fluctuation, risk), the higher the return. In other words, no pain, no gain. This is also the reason why money market funds result in such a low return. They never go below zero (at least so far!) or lose value. Therefore, they are as low risk as you can get. Unfortunately, they are also currently about as low in returns as you can get. As of this writing, money market funds were yielding close to 4.00 percent. Yes, there is no "risk" to speak of and your account will not lose value, but how many can survive with that kind of return? After inflation and income taxes, you actually are **guaranteed** to lose money at this rate of return. Also, using the "Rule of 72," it would take approximately eighteen years to double your money before you even consider taxes and inflation. With those two items factored in, it will probably take twice that amount of time, if not more. Small-cap stocks, with their higher risk, have returned an average of 12 percent annually since 1927. In other words, small-cap stocks double every six years on average. Thus, using the Rule of 72, one can see that small-cap stocks would be four times what the money market funds (or CD's, for that matter) would be after twenty-four years.

Let me give you an idea about diversification here. If you allocated 50 percent to a money market fund and 50 percent to small-cap stocks, you would have received an average return of 7.5 percent. By diversifying between these two assets, you have increased the return from just the money market funds and reduced the risk from just the small-cap stocks. In real life, that is how asset allocation works.

The bottom line is that you want to be able to measure the risk/reward ratio in conjunction with your investment plan. Ask yourself, "How much income do I need and how much risk can I afford to take without jeopardizing the success of my financial plan?" Too many people have learned hard lessons by jumping in and taking a great risk on a very volatile investment, only to realize how great the risk was after losing their shirts.

If greater risk generates greater rewards, why shouldn't every one just invest in the investment with the greatest risk? Because the fluctuations (volatility) would drive you crazy. It would be exhilarating to see the investment go up in value but, when it drops, would you have the courage of your convictions to stay the course through all the stomach turning that you would inevitably experience as it keeps going down while you wait for it to come back up? Besides, what if you were wrong and the investment never recovered, or, gasp, it went to zero (like Enron or WorldCom stock)? **It would be a good idea to figure out what your risk tolerance is before you jump into risky ventures**. Yes, the potential for higher return may be there, but will your risk tolerance allow you to stay the course when the market turns against you? Be honest when you answer this because your ability to reach, and stay on Golden Pond depends on it.

Diversification through proper allocation among various asset classes is probably one of the best ways of assuring that you will do so in the long run. I mention "the long run" because for any given month, quarter or year, there will be fluctuations and you must allow time for the investment to work for you. If your child is going to college next year, or if you are thinking of buying a house in the near future, you should not be putting that money into any investment that has the potential of losing principal in the short run, no matter how terrific your asset allocation program is.

7. Overstaying Your Welcome

Don't you hate it when someone comes over and doesn't know when to leave? Everything has gone well, you've enjoyed a delicious meal, you've shared desert and coffee, swapped great stories, and had some laughs, but they simply don't know when to go home. After a wonderful evening, it all goes sour when you practically have to kick them out, leaving your friendship on shaky ground. I remember reading an expression that summarizes the situation completely: guests, like fish, begin to stink after a while. That's so true!

People do this with investments all of the time. While this applies more to individual stock, bond, or mutual fund investments, it can apply equally well to a diversified asset allocation portfolio and the need for rebalancing among the various asset classes by selling the winners and putting the proceeds into assets that have not done as well. This basically pertains to all investors who are reluctant to sell for whatever reason and wind up with portfolios that are skewed towards higher risk than their tolerance dictates.

They have gotten into these investments after having studied them carefully (I am giving them the benefit of doubt on this one) and with great enthusiasm. They are fortunate enough to see good results. The party has gone nicely, and they've even exceeded their growth expectations from the investment. But then the investment starts to slow down a bit. Just as the ticking clock shows it's getting later in the evening, perhaps the business behind the investment has lost its edge in the market. Yet, somehow, you just can't come to grips with the fact that it's time to get out—the party's over, and it's time to leave.

Why do people stay too long? Some do so because they are greedy. They figure there's always a little more coming up if they just wait. Some of them don't know when to be satisfied and walk away and reposition their profits into investments that have not done as well (remember: buy low, sell high to take advantage of market cycles). Some people have a great aversion to paying taxes on their capital gains.

This reluctance to sell also applies to people who have seen their investments decline in value. In a way, they are similar to the people who go to Las Vegas, get in a hole, and keep doubling up thinking their luck has to change sooner or later. Many people hang onto some investments that they should have gotten out of long ago. Yes, holding onto stocks over the long-run is a way to make money, but sometimes it is simply time to call it quits and get out.

For a great many others, it's a matter of not being able to admit they are wrong. They fool themselves with the misguided belief that someday the stock will turn around. But a dog is a dog is a dog, and sometimes you simply have to face reality and move on. If you don't have some information about the company that supports the idea of holding onto the stock or mutual fund, then why stay put? Your money could be doing better elsewhere (that's called "opportunity cost," i.e. the money you lose by not being in another, more profitable investment while you are waiting for the current investment to go up in value). Just like a bad marriage or a dead end job, sometimes you simply have to say, "It's time to get out."

Buying the right stock at the right price and getting out at the right time and the right price is based more on luck than on skill, and it really should not be counted on to get you to Golden Pond. Believe me, you are much better off with a well-diversified portfolio comprised of various asset classes in proportion to your particular risk tolerance and financial objectives.

8. Ignorance

The old saying, "ignorance is bliss," does not pertain to investing. Far from it. Too many people follow the advice of others and invest in areas that they know absolutely nothing about. Commodities and futures, for example, are investments that most people do not have the foggiest idea about, much less understand. Therefore, they should not be putting their money into such risky investments. Even the stock market can be tricky. The introduction of online trading didn't stop many investors from jumping right in, not knowing very much about stocks other than what a friend told them or an article reported. "How hard can it be to invest?" asked the wide-eyed new investor, who, with a few clicks of the mouse, was suddenly a day trader. I remember those days of the "dot-com" mania. There was never a day when I did not come across people who were going to, or already had, quit their regular jobs to become day traders and pursue the American dream. Instead of a dream, the people that acted on this urge had one gigantic nightmare.

The reality is that investing takes due diligence. You need to take the time to do the research. The Internet provides a great tool for learning about the stock market, mutual funds, bonds, and even commodities and futures. Articles abound detailing what each type of investment is all about. Unfortunately, in the late nineties, rather than read about investments, too many people thought it was more fun to go onto the Internet and start buying and selling like they were playing a computer game. Rather than doing the research, they preferred to play. The only difference was that they were playing the game with real money. Even with research, it is difficult to make money in individual stocks. But without research, you are doomed to fail in the long run. Sure, you could luck out once in a while. However, ask yourself if you really want to count on just luck to make it to Golden Pond. For your sake, I hope the answer is a resounding "**No!**" The easy accessibility of investing from the comfort of one's own home made it too easy for people to get into the market without understanding the market at all, and that's always a big mistake. **You need to understand any investment opportunity before putting your money into it.** To use the old cliché, **Investigate before you Invest!** Remember this when someone (like a broker) says, "Don't worry, you don't need to understand it, that's my job." No way. **It's your job too!**

Keep in mind that Wall Street has thousands of analysts with lots of education, lots of experience, and a lot more resources than you will ever have right there at their finger tips. If they succeed only once in a while, how can you really expect to beat the odds that are so heavily stacked against you?

9. Paying too much in fees, commissions

I am a little biased in this regard, but I just cannot see buying front-end loaded mutual funds, or any kind of load, if I can help it. Load is the commission that the mutual fund company charges you just to buy into their product. For example, in a 5 percent front-end loaded fund, your $1000 investment is immediately worth $950 because the company took $50 to pay a commission to the salesman that sold you the product and keep some for itself. Now you have to make approximately 6 percent just to break even, and if the investment goes south for a while, you are in an even bigger hole. Then there are management fees that are disclosed in the prospectus (but nobody ever reads them, right?). These could range anywhere from 0.25 percent to 1.5 percent, or even 2 percent annually! **Loads and management fees certainly help your broker and the mutual fund company, but they have a negative impact on your rate of return**.

A similar case could be made for buying/selling stocks. In the 1983 movie *Trading Places*, Mortimer and Randolph (played by Don Ameche and Ralph Bellamy) are the co-owners of a commodities firm. They tell Billy Ray (played by Eddie Murphy), a broker on the first day at his new job, "We make money when the market goes up, and we make money when the market goes down." To this, Billy Ray replies, "You guys are just like bookies!" In this day of $9.99 or less per trade on the Internet, I find it amazing that "full service" brokerages charge the commissions they do. In the old days, they used to justify it by offering you "research," but today that research is readily available on the Internet. The research that these firms provide are full of conflicts of interest, and the content of the report is already reflected in the price of the stock by the time you read it (this is called "efficient market hypothesis" in financial circles). If you can do the investing yourself, you might be better off, but if you can't, try to negotiate a better rate. The money you save on fees and commissions has a direct bearing on how much faster you can get to Golden Pond.

10. Trusting Institutions

That interaction between Mortimer, Randolph, and Billy Ray that I mentioned in the previous paragraph tells it all. **Always keep in mind that the primary goal of an institution is to gather assets and make lots of money for themselves**. Your goals are of secondary importance and sometimes may even represent a conflict of interest for the broker. After all, if his paycheck depends on his ability to persuade you to buy or sell, what is he supposed to tell you? If you don't buy or sell (he doesn't care which one you do so long as you do something to generate a commission or fee), he cannot make any money. Often, he could also be in danger of losing his job because he could not meet the company's quota. More often, he will be given a lower payout if the commissions he generates for his company drops below a certain level. And if it drops even further, he will find himself on the street without a job. Do you think he wants to risk that?

I don't care how sincere the television commercial may sound; the people behind the commercial are trying to make money—not for you, but for them. The same holds true for the many financial experts (on TV, in magazines, at seminars, wherever) who are touting new ways in which you can become a millionaire. If someone really had a way by which you could "get rich overnight," why would he sell his secret for a few hundred or thousand dollars? It doesn't make sense, does it?

Too often, we base our trust in someone who is out for a commission and not looking out for our best interests. I must admit that years ago I did this for my own account and lost a few thousand dollars in the process by dabbling in commodities. I got conned into an investment before I knew what it was all about. I trusted someone, and I shouldn't have.

It is extremely important that you place your trust in someone you know, trust, and believe in. To do this, you need to do some homework, learn a little bit about the various investments, and learn about the person who will help you invest. Remember, "investigate before you invest" applies to advisors, brokers, and institutions just as it does for individual, specific investments.

You should approach a financial advisor (or stockbroker) not as someone to whom you will simply hand over your money to manage, but as someone you are interviewing to work with you—to help you and to guide you.

The idea that every financial advisor, stockbroker, or financial institution will do right by you is very naïve thinking. Just as you should have good recommendations about a doctor and have questions ready when you visit his or her office, you should approach any financial professional in the same manner, whether it's someone working in a small home-office or a major financial institution. If you don't feel comfortable, and you do not believe that he or she will work in your best interest, do not sign anything and walk away.

The reality is that financial brokers are looking to make a commission off of your business. There is nothing wrong with that. But what is he doing to earn it? Is he entitled to it? You need to determine to what degree this person is taking **your needs** into account. Is he asking you questions and trying to determine what is best for you? Or is he trying to sell you on an investment vehicle the minute you sit down in the office? It is amazing how many people will blindly follow whatever a financial professional tells them because, after all, he is in the field, so he must be right. But think about this, how can he be right if he doesn't don't know what your goals or needs are? How can he have any idea what to sell you (and, believe me, they are selling!) if he doesn't know you, doesn't know your level of risk tolerance, and doesn't know what asset allocation is best for you?

How can he have the perfect investment (chosen just for you) ready to whip out of his drawer and show you five minutes after you walk in his office? It's no different than when someone calls you on the telephone, doesn't even know how to pronounce your name, and then tries to sell you something. Does this person know you at all? Of course not. Would you trust them with your life savings? Of course not.

Don't follow the advice of any financial professional unless you believe in this person and feel that he has taken an interest in you and your long-term financial picture. It's very easy for a broker, or even an advisor, to sell you something, take a commission, and then six months later say, "Oops, sorry it didn't work out." He's not losing a thing (except maybe a client), but you are. In short, he is selling you up the river without a paddle, and this is not helping you get to your Golden Pond. Hey, perhaps he is counting on you to help him get to his Golden Pond!

You also want to know who will be handling your account. In many of the large firms, one person brings you in, and then they hand your account over to some account manager who doesn't know you from Adam. Here, you've gone and put your trust in someone who has handed it over to someone else. This happens frequently at the large financial companies where you can easily get lost in the shuffle. There are stories of people calling up a large brokerage house and speaking to account managers who are not even able to locate the person's accounts, much less manage them properly.

Get recommendations before you sit down with a financial advisor or stockbroker. Then make sure he or she is the person with whom you will be working and that you will not be passed along to a virtual stranger. **And finally, remember that no one has all of the answers; if he did, he'd be on a beach in the Bahamas. He would certainly not be working, trying to help you with your financial concerns.**

11. Not being "money smart"

As mentioned previously in this chapter, there are people who absolutely refuse to sell any investment at a loss. These people will keep hanging on to a stock that is losing money, waiting for that magical day when they will "break even" and then get out. Once in a while they may luck out. Often times, it does not work out, and all they succeed in doing is turning a small loss into a big one. Besides, even if they do succeed in "breaking even," they have spent all their time and energy holding on to something when they could have been much better off in a better investment that had a higher potential for profit.

Similarly, not keeping accurate records, not knowing the exact cost of the investment (purchase price plus interest charges, if you borrowed money to invest), and not understanding the tax ramifications of your investment decisions are all factors that can cause you to make decisions that could come back to haunt you and prevent you from reaching Golden Pond.

12. Accepting advice from amateurs

Just because a neighbor or a friend claims to have made money in a particular investment does not make him an expert in investments. Even so, thousands of people fall prey to "tips" provided by these amateurs who were lucky enough to find a winner. This also pertains to people who may be experts in a totally unrelated field, but because of their success in that field, are looked upon as great sources of investment wisdom.

Usually by the time you act on the "tip," it's too late, and you often find yourself losing money by following the advice of people who really do not know much more than you do. **Most of the time, hot tips only wind up burning you**. More seriously, you sometimes take financial advice on matters pertaining to other areas of your personal finances (e.g. legal) thinking you are saving on the fees you would have paid a professional. In such a case, if the advice turns out to be incorrect, the cost ramifications of the error could be several times the fee you would have paid a qualified professional.

13. Accepting as gospel the recommendations from brokerages and the media

The brokerage's primary purpose is to get new customers and make more money, while the media's primary purpose is to get more viewers (or subscribers) and make more money. Both of these goals come at your expense. If they can perhaps make you money while they are trying to achieve the primary purpose of their existence, fine. But the sooner you realize that you are secondary to them, the better off you will be. Read up or listen to any and all investment ideas promoted by these sources with a grain of salt. Before you blindly accept their word, do a little research on your own. So if you read in a magazine about "Six great stocks to buy today," it doesn't mean that you have to go right out and buy them immediately. Take your time, do your own research, analyze your own risk tolerance and investment objectives, and only after you are convinced that the stock(s) is right for you, invest **at the appropriate time.**

14. Chasing performance

No one investment advisor or money manager can consistently be on top of the performance heap. This is why you try to diversify and use asset allocation with your investment strategy. Yet most people will try to invest in the top performer at that moment, only to find that they are too late. Even if the hot performer may eventually perform well again, they usually go through a correction before they resume their performance. The correction usually shakes out the performance-chasing investor, who sells out at a loss because now there is something else that's performing well. If you keep repeating this cycle of "buy high, sell low," often enough, you will find yourself poorer, but not necessarily wiser. **Investment discipline—having the courage of your convictions and staying the course—is in short supply in today's instant-gratification world**. Again, proper asset allocation and diversification is of tremendous value in trying to overcome this pitfall.

15. Trying to time the market

If you are not a professional trader, getting in and out of the market completely based on short-term changes will only wind up making you poorer. Even professional traders are not very successful at this, so what makes you think you can be good at it? If you persist in doing so, you will be making decisions based on emotions that are dictated by the day. You will wind up getting whipsawed—buying high and selling low constantly. **You will find yourself Up The Creek with this approach, I guarantee you!**

However, based on changes in your personal circumstances, your risk tolerance and your objectives, you should, and are expected to adjust your portfolio. For example, if your portfolio allocation originally called for 80 percent growth (stocks) and 20 percent fixed income (bonds) (80/20) or some such percentage, and you realize that you are now just a couple of years away from retirement, you may decide to lower the risk in your portfolio by changing the allocation to 70/30 or 60/40. **It is essential that you not change the allocation just because you have seen that stocks are doing well currently, and so you decide to adjust your portfolio to get**

higher returns. In this latter case, you are chasing returns and that is never a good idea.

Tweaking or adjusting your portfolio periodically is necessary to maintain the health of your portfolio. This is similar to weeding your garden to maintain the health of your landscaping. For example, if your portfolio consisted of an asset class, say, large-cap growth, which had an original allocation of 15 percent based on your risk tolerance and objectives, and it is currently at 20 percent, you may decide to sell the extra 5 percent and reposition the proceeds into an asset class that has dropped in value. This periodic "tweaking" will ensure that your portfolio is in sync with your risk tolerance and objectives at all times.

16. Falling in love with your investments

Remember: it's okay to date a stock or investment, but it's not okay to marry it. If the stock or investment begins to falter, cut the cord and get out. In the late nineties, a lot of people fell in love with their technology stocks and refused to sell until it was just too late and the stocks had dropped 80 percent or more from their highs. Some people kept buying more as the prices went down only to watch helplessly as the stocks went down even further. Just keep in mind, that **the market really doesn't care whether you are in love with a stock or not or.** Once you realize that conditions have changed since you bought it, get out. **Never, ever overstay your welcome.**

17. Checking your portfolio value too often

Of all the things that cause one to make the wrong investment decision, this has got to be among the most common. There is a truism on Wall Street: your holding period is directly proportional to the frequency with which you check the value of your portfolio. If you are investing for the long term, why would you focus on short-term performance?

As I have mentioned elsewhere in this book, at any given time, fear or greed can dictate your investment decisions. Greed dictates your decisions when it comes to buying, and fear kicks in when it comes to selling. The human mind is such that you look upon the latest *event du jour* as the first one of its kind, and as such, it will either make you a millionaire overnight or it will cause you to lose everything.

The safest antidote to this problem is to check your accounts periodically, mainly to make sure that your account is still properly diversified in relation to your risk tolerance and objectives. Of course, if you are speculating instead of investing for the long term, you will be tossed this way and that way, zigging when you should be zagging, getting whipsawed, buying high and selling low every time the markets move suddenly up or down. In that case, I can assure you that you will be making decisions in the heat of the moment—decisions that will affect you adversely in the long run. Please, do yourself a favor; do not check you accounts every day. Once a week would be just fine, as long as you have taken a structured, disciplined approach to investing for your future through proper diversification and asset allocation in keeping with your risk tolerance and objectives.

Here is a suggestion for you: before you panic and act in the heat of the moment, try to determine if the drop has really affected your ability to get to (or stay on) Golden Pond. If it hasn't, you really don't need to act. If it has, try to decide what adjustment to your portfolio will help you get back on track. This is true especially when your account has dropped in value. In this regard, the process of Monte Carlo Simulation is an invaluable tool. However, since most readers will not have access to that tool, I suggest that you take a step back and try not to act on the spur of the moment. I have yet to see actions triggered by panic work out. They usually do a lot more harm than good.

18. You are not in sync with your spouse's objectives and risk tolerance

Many investors do not get their spouses involved in their investment decisions. Their belief is that the wife will not understand what they are doing, and they will therefore impede their decision making. In my experience, men are more guilty of this than women. Sometimes it is because they are the sole income earners in the family. Most often, it is because men believe that "she just would not understand." I have seen men take ridiculous risks without their spouse's knowledge, involvement or approval, figuring "what they don't know won't hurt them." Nothing could be further from the truth.

The journey to "Golden Pond" is a joint venture, and one spouse's financial decisions have the potential to impact the other spouse's ability to reach that destination. I know of occasions where one spouse has been devastated by the realization (often too late) that the other spouse borrowed too much, over-used the credit cards, or took such inappropriate risks that they are now further behind on the road to Golden Pond than when they began their journey. **You owe it to your spouse** to tell him or her what is going on and to get them involved in the process. I have mentioned wives as the victims in this case because that has been my experience, but there is no reason why this would not apply to women getting their husbands involved, either. This was a common problem when it came time to file tax returns, and it is the main reason why we now have an "Innocent Spouse Rule."

19. Not understanding how investments work: not educating yourself

Even if you hire a professional, but even more so if you invest on your own, do yourself a huge favor. Try to familiarize yourself with various types of investments by reading books, attending seminars or workshops, etc. More importantly, read business publications (e.g. *The Wall Street Journal* or the business section of your daily newspaper) to get a feel for what is happening in the country and in the world, in general. A better understanding of the markets will lead to better decisions. Most importantly, it will also help you determine realistic goals and manage your expectations.

20. Letting past investment decisions/experiences affect today's decisions

No situation is exactly the same as one in the past. Each one is unique in terms of your own personal circumstances as well as external circumstances, such as the condition of the domestic or global economy, interest rates, unemployment, etc.

The market has a way of confounding even the biggest experts. So while you can use your past experience to arrive at a buy/sell/hold decision, **you cannot blindly base a decision on what happened in the past.** Remember, **it's the market's job to make sure that the majority of the people are wrong a majority of the time.** The moment you get cocky and begin to think you have figured out how the market works, you will be in danger of making your worst decisions. Everyone, regardless of experience, makes mistakes. Over time, your expectation should be that you will make fewer "big" mistakes. Your past experiences are good for just that and no more. **Investing is an on-going, never-ending process where no one ever really makes all the right decisions, all of the time.**

21. Losing sight of your goals, objectives, and risk tolerance.

There is an expression which goes something like this: **when you are up to your rear end in alligators, you forget that your first task is to drain the swamp.** In other words, you might be prone to acting rashly in the heat of the moment. You might turn on the TV or radio and discover that some event somewhere in the USA (or perhaps half way across the world) has caused the market to drop, say, two hundred points. Without taking a step back to analyze the ramifications of such an event, you panic and sell all of the investments you own, only to realize much later that the temporary drop may have been an excellent buying opportunity.

In some respects this is similar to #17 ("Checking your portfolio value too often"). It really pays to know your risk tolerance, what you are trying to do with your investments, and the long-term ramifications of a sudden drop in your portfolio. That is the reason why it pays to **write** down your investment goals and objectives.

22. Not taking taxes, transaction costs, and inflation into consideration

Remember: **It's not what you make that matters; it's what you get to keep.** It is relatively easy to factor in the taxes and transaction cost, but you also have to take into account the cost of inflation to determine if you are truly better off. For example, during the Jimmy Carter era, a lot of people liked the fact that they were getting double-digit returns on their Certificates of Deposit. But people who put their money (notice I did not say "invest." That's because I consider CDs to be a place to park your money temporarily) into CDs failed to consider the effects of inflation, which was around 12 percent at the time! On an after-tax, after-inflation basis, they were negative. Yet, they were happy in the belief that they were making a killing on their CDs despite the fact that they were the ones getting killed.

23. Looking for perfection and certainty

Let me rephrase the hypothetical question I asked in Chapter 2: if you were supposed to attend an event a couple of miles from your house, but decided not to start your car until every traffic light between your house and the destination was green, when would you be able to start?

Perhaps never, right? So, why is it that people always have to look for everything to be just perfect before they will take any action? **The sooner you accept the fact that the traffic lights in your life are never going to be all green, the sooner you can start making meaningful advances towards your goals.** Sure, you are going to make mistakes, but the trick is in keeping the losses small and learning from your mistakes. I am no psychologist, but I believe that waiting for everything to be just right before you do anything is a manner of stalling because you are afraid to make a decision and act. If that is the case with you, you might not want to admit it to anyone, even yourself. But if you are honest about it, you will realize that perhaps you are better off hiring someone to make the decisions and act on your behalf.

24. Hiring the wrong professional

Just like people chase after the hottest stocks, some people chase after the hottest money manager. Remember, there is a huge difference between a money manager and a financial advisor who also manages your money. All the money manager does is try to manage your portfolio according to your specifications. The financial advisor is the one who knows about your personal circumstances and your life objectives and has the ability to guide you through the myriad of financial complexities, such as income taxes, estate planning, funding for college, etc. The financial advisor is the one who is reviewing your progress as you make your way to Golden Pond. He is the one who recommends corrective action when necessary. Of course, a person can always have a financial advisor who does not manage money for the overall steering of the ship, while having a money manager do the investing. Just know what you are most comfortable with and choose the appropriate one for the right reasons. Keep in mind that last quarter's performance is NOT a good reason to choose or reject a professional.

25. Not enjoying the journey

I admit that this particular mistake is not going to impact your ability to get to Golden Pond, but let's face it; it's going to take years before you achieve your objective. I do not want you to become so obsessed with the ultimate goal that you totally forget to live and enjoy life along the way. So when you are setting up your goals and objectives, be sure to allocate some time and money for enjoyment of life; just make sure you do not make it the highest priority. You should seek a balance between the current enjoyment of life and your future retirement security.

Chapter 8

Retirement Plans

IN THIS CHAPTER, I look at some of the ways in which you can plan for your retirement and examine some of the common pitfalls. It's been said that retirement is like a three-legged stool. One leg is your employer, which typically includes the company's retirement plan or benefits (a 401(k) plan, which includes the new Roth 401(k)), a pension plan, or a profit sharing plan. The second leg is the government, which consists primarily of social security payments. The third leg—the one that plays the most important role—is you. This is the only leg that you can really count on. In a way, even the company's 401(k) plan could be considered part of you, but the others—the pension, the social security, etc, cannot really be counted on to be there for you when you need them. So, as the saying goes, "if it's got to be, it's up to me!" This chapter will focus on how you can ensure your own retirement security without being overly dependent on your employer, the government, or even your family and friends.

Your Employer: Company Retirement Plans

A. 401(k) plans

Since their inception in 1981, company-offered 401(k) plans have become very attractive. They have provided an easy means of saving for retirement. Employers essentially set up the program, and if you choose to participate, your money is transferred directly into it from your paycheck. You can determine how much you choose to contribute and select investment options. Most companies have a waiting period until you are eligible to enroll in a 401(k) plan. The company typically matches some percentage of your contributions, and, because it's a retirement plan, this money is tax-deferred. It's typically advantageous to take part in a 401(k) plan if one is offered by your company.

I find it totally amazing that, in spite of the benefits of tax-deferral and company matching, so many people decide not to participate in the 401(k) program offered by their employers. Granted, some people may have difficulty meeting their monthly expenses and may need all the cash flow they can get, but, if that's the case, they should seriously attempt to cut down on some other expenses to try and participate in the program. **Participating in a 401(k) plan is one of the best financial moves you can make**—you get to defer your income tax on the contribution (assuming it's not a Roth 401(k)) for the year, as well as the growth of that contribution until such time as you withdraw money from the account at retirement. In this plan, you can salt away as much as $15,000 in 2006, and if you are over age fifty, you get to put in an additional $5,000—a total of $20,000, if your cash flow permits it.

Some companies offer profit-sharing plans, where employers make discretionary contributions, which may vary from year to year. The success and profits of the business will determine the amount of the contributions that are made. By law, a profit-sharing plan must have a definite formula allocating the contributions for each participant. Some plans have "vesting" requirements, i.e. the company's contributions to your plan only become yours after a specified period of time. Profit-sharing plans are rapidly being replaced by 401(k) plans due to the fact that the latter requires a lower outlay on the part of the employer, and shifts the onus to the employee.

Pension plans are also much less common than in the past. Twenty to thirty years ago, many companies had such plans whereby the longer you worked for a company, the more vesting you built up toward the pension plan. Once you were 100 percent vested, you would be due your money upon retirement, either in the form of a monthly annuity or, in rare cases, a lump sum distribution that could be rolled over to your IRA. The amount you received would be calculated based on the number of years you had worked for the company and your salary during the last few years of employment. Today, you may not have a pension plan, as most companies have done away with them. If there is such a plan offered by your company, the employee benefits department or the union to which you belong can apprise you of where you stand in regard to your pension benefits. While most employers do not allow lump-sum distributions from their pension plans, they do allow it for profit sharing and 401(k) plans. You are then entitled to take a lump-sum payment and then roll it over into your IRA. In this case, you decide to annuitize your plan at retirement; i.e. to take monthly payments. **If you are married, note that it is absolutely essential that you take it as a "joint" payment with your spouse.** In fact, you will not be allowed to take the monthly payment just based on your own life expectancy without the signed consent of the spouse. Most people get lured by the higher payment of the annuity based on just their own life. In a way, the retiree is gambling that he will outlive his wife. But, what happens if his wife outlives him? In that case, she is left without any benefits whatsoever.

It doesn't matter whether you take an option that pays the surviving spouse 100 percent, 75 percent, or 50 percent of the payment you were receiving while both of you were alive. This can be decided on with some discussion between you and your spouse; **but please, do not get tempted by the higher payment of the annuity based on one life alone.**

A great strategy!

There is strategy worth considering. You could take the higher payment (with your spouse's signed consent) and use the difference (the higher payment based on one life minus the lower payment based on two lives) to buy life insurance for the surviving spouse. An added advantage to this approach is that the life insurance proceeds could be passed on to the children or other beneficiaries if the spouse was no longer alive to receive the payments (even with joint annuities, the annuity payments, in general, stop after the surviving spouse dies). However, you have to make sure that the premiums are low enough to make the move worthwhile. In other words, the retiree must be in relatively good health and insurable. There are a lot of nuances to this strategy, but it's definitely something to consider before you opt for an annuity from your employer.

A potential land mine!

One word of warning in case you decide to take a lump sum distribution: <u>never, ever</u> have the check made payable to you. You could find that the payment is considered a distribution and 20 percent of the total amount is automatically withheld for federal income taxes. Even if you do roll over the remaining 80 percent to your IRA, the other 20 percent will be considered a distribution and be subject to taxation! Of course, you can take the exact amount that was withheld for taxes from your own checking, saving or investment account and deposit that amount with the other 80 percent in to the IRA. In that case, you would be refunded the 20 percent at tax return time. However, usually people do not have that kind of money lying around to be able to do that, especially if it happens to be substantial. Plus, the hassle involved, even if you do have the money on the side to make the deposit, makes it something to avoid. Believe me, **the best option is to open an IRA rollover account with an institutional custodian and have the lump sum distribution check made payable to the custodian for benefit of your account at that institution**. By doing this, you avoid all of the potential problems.

B. Stock purchase plans

Another company option may be to allow purchase of company stock at a discount (perhaps 15 percent). This can be beneficial, but as is typically the case with stocks, there is a greater risk. You also can be subject to capital gains taxes, which makes this option less attractive. I know of people who have made a career of buying their company stock at a discount, and then turning around and selling it for a quick profit, regardless of the fact that the gain is considered "short-term" (if holding period is less than 12 months) and, therefore, considered ordinary income. Why do we have to know this? Because long-term capital gains are, in most cases, taxed at a much more favorable rate than short-term capital gains and ordinary, earned income.

If your company does offer its stock for sale to its employees at a discounted price, buying in limited amounts can be a worthwhile investment, considering the risk typically associated with stock investments.

Major pitfalls of company retirement plans

There are two major pitfalls pertaining to company retirement plans you should be aware of. They are:

1. Investing too heavily in your company stock.

The availability and discount on company stock makes it tempting to "stock up" so to speak. The tenuous state of the stock market, however, indicates that you should not invest too heavily in any one company, not even the one you work for. You should limit your investment in your company's stock to no more than 10 percent of your portfolio. Diversification is still important to your retirement planning, and even as a loyal employee you need to exercise good judgment when buying company stock.

This also applies to overloading your 401(k) plan with company stock, either out of a false sense of loyalty to the company, or because you think you are going to make a killing. Remember Enron. The employees of that company found out too late how dangerous it can be to invest in company stock. Sometimes, as in the case of Enron, your company might force you to invest in company stock. Beware of this; it's a jungle out there. Overloading your retirement with company stock has the potential to sink the boat that you thought was going to get you to Golden Pond.

2. Ignoring your 401(k) plan

While the act of simply enrolling in a 401(k) plan is a giant step in the right direction, the vast majority of people contributing to 401(k) plans completely forget that they have options and can change their investments within the plan in accordance with personal goals and market conditions. To make a plan really work for you, it is important to stay on top of your investments and make adjustments when necessary. It's astonishing how many people do not ever do this. The 401(k) should be treated just like your regular portfolio. You need to diversify, allocate among various choices (based on asset classes), and monitor the account to ensure that the risk within the account does not get out of hand. Do not ever chase performance in this account. **Remember, the 401(k) is a marathon, not a sprint.**

Beginning in 2006, we have a new wrinkle in the 401(k) scene. You now have the option of setting aside part of your salary in a Roth 401(k) plan. With the regular plan, you are able to defer taxes on the amount contributed until you make withdrawals from that 401(k) (or one that has been rolled over to an IRA). However, with a Roth 401(k), you pay income tax currently on the money you contribute, with the understanding that that contribution and the growth associated with it will never be taxed at withdrawal. So, if your employer does offer both types of 401(k)s, you will need to decide how much of the contribution to allocate to each type of 401(k). You may decide to take the tax deduction up front and pay taxes later at withdrawal with the regular 401(k), or you may decide to pay taxes currently and let the contributions accumulate totally tax-free. The choice is entirely based on what your individual circumstances are. However, **it is imperative that you make regular monthly contributions to one or both types of 401(k)s.**

The Government

Social Security followed the uneasy times of the Great Depression. It was created in the mid-thirties to insure that seniors were taken care of by the government. Nearly seventy years later, some fifty million people collect Social Security. When Social Security was started back in 1935, life expectancy was sixty-three, and the age at which you could start to collect Social Security was sixty-five. The government figured most people would be dead by the age of sixty-five, and those who were not dead could collect from the government for only a short while. **At the time Social Security was started, only one person was collecting Social Security for every forty-five working people.**

Over the years, however, life expectancy has increased dramatically (today, it is approximately seventy-eight for men and eighty-two for women), but the age at which you can collect has increased only slightly to sixty-seven, and the ratio of individuals working to those collecting Social Security is less than three to one. Millions of people today are collecting Social Security. Add up all those facts, and it does not take a genius to figure out that the well is about to run dry if some drastic measures are not undertaken.

Left on its own, the system as it exists today, just cannot last much longer. The minimum age for collecting will have to be increased, or the system will need to be completely overhauled if Social Security is going to survive to benefit future generations. There is much debate in Congress on how to keep Social Security afloat, and many more changes may be in store between now and the time you are eligible to collect.

Therefore, **the biggest pitfall regarding Social Security is counting on it to take care of you in your retirement years**. Even today, when it is supposedly more solvent than what it might be in the future, the reality is that at most, you can receive about $22,000 per year. Moreover, under certain circumstances, 85 percent of what you receive from Social Security could be subject to federal and, in certain states, even state income taxation.

Remember, even when Social Security was created more than seventy years ago, **it was never intended to be the only source of income for retirees.** It was intended to be a supplement to the other sources of income during retirement. Somewhere along the line, people got to believing that the government would take care of them during old age and therefore decided not to take any action to provide for their own retirement security. These are the people who now find themselves truly Up The Creek!

Keep this firmly in mind as you make your way towards your Golden Pond. It is best not to count on Social Security for your retirement needs. Assuming it is still around when you retire, it will only provide a small percentage of your retirement income needs. The rest will be up to you and, maybe, your employer. Also keep in mind that changes to the system, for better or worse, are on the horizon.

You!

Obviously the strongest leg of your retirement plan will have to be you and your own resources. While a 401(k) plan is advisable and good for you, and Social Security can provide a small portion of your retirement income, the reality is that you need to start making your own investment plans. **The notion that your company and your government will take care of you is no longer valid.** You will have to act as your own Santa Claus, folks. And the sooner you realize that fact and accept it, the sooner you can start making plans and undertaking actions that will get you to the Promised Land (Golden Pond). Okay, I realize that ponds do not have land. So, make it promised water, but start taking responsibility for your own future, will you?

Individual Retirement Accounts (IRA's)

Both Roth and traditional IRA's are a popular starting point for saving for retirement. Deciding whether you want to take the tax hit now or pay taxes upon withdrawing the money will help you determine which type of IRA you want to use. The traditional IRA is a tax-deferred investment. The Roth IRA, however, now just over eight years old, has gained a lot of attention from a population that is living and working longer. A Roth IRA is not a tax-deferred investment per se. Even though you do not get a tax deduction for your contribution to your Roth IRA, the growth of that account will **never** be taxed, assuming certain rules are followed. That means that you will pay taxes on the money you put into the Roth, but you will be able to withdraw money tax-free at a later date, probably at retirement time when you may have a higher income then previous generations of retirees. The Roth 401(k) is a by-product of this savings tool.

There are also no age limits for a Roth IRA, allowing you to make contributions for as long as you choose. The contribution limit for an IRA is $4,000 for 2006 ($4,500 if you are age fifty or above). However, if you are self-employed, under certain circumstances you can contribute $42,000 to your Simplified Employee Pension Plan, commonly referred to as a SEP/IRA. This is a fabulous way for some self-employed individuals to salt away significant money for their trip to Golden Pond.

The Pitfalls

While many are identical to the Barriers to Golden Pond listed in Chapter 2, some of those pitfalls are worth repeating at this time. The pitfalls that people commonly fall into while planning their own leg of the three-legged retirement stool are:

1. Investing too heavily in tax-deferred accounts.

You should make sure that you're not overly-invested in tax-deferred accounts, or you may find yourself paying a lot of taxes later on when you need the money for retirement. The idea of deferring taxes is based on the notion that after you retire, your income taxes will be lower than while you are working. However, the amount that accumulates in the retirement plan can be substantial. That, combined with people starting their own businesses, investing in more diverse areas, and in some cases, taking on new jobs after their official "retirement," can make the income substantially higher after retirement. In this scenario, the tax bite can be significant. Therefore, you should try to maintain a balance between tax-deferred and non tax-deferred savings.

2. Following the wrong person.

While friends, co-workers, neighbors, and relatives may have the best of intentions; it is not their money that you are investing;

it is yours. Therefore, you need to invest in conjunction with **your** goals and needs. Too many people follow bad advice and invest in something that was right for someone else and not for them. Even magazines and online investment recommendations may be wrong for you. Remember, just like your taste in food, cars, or clothing, an investment has to suit you, not someone else.

3. Procrastination, or starting too late

Procrastination is your enemy when trying to build your nest egg for retirement. The longer you wait to start saving, the more you will need to put away to accumulate a significant amount of money on which to retire. Refer back to **Exhibit 2-9** for a refresher. If you are twenty-five years old and you want to have a million dollars by the time you are sixty-five, you need to invest $2,055 annually at a rate of 10 percent per year. But if you wait ten years, until you are age thirty-five, before you begin your investment program, you will need to put aside $5,527 annually. And, by gosh, if you decide to start at age of forty-five, you will not only need to invest $12,392 annually, but you will also need to make 12 percent annually on that money. See why procrastination is such a big problem? **The earlier you start working toward your goal of Golden Pond, the faster you're going to reach it and the longer you can stay on it.**

Unfortunately, many people don't start even thinking retirement until they are forty-five or fifty-five, and it's very hard to save up enough money when you start that late. In addition, by starting later, you can't afford to make too many mistakes with your nest egg. The more you realize how much you need to save, the more you realize you cannot afford to take chances because there is no one to look after you but yourself.

4. Assuming that your children will support you after you have retired.

While it is wonderful if your children are in a position to help you out, it is certainly not something you can count on. A common pitfall in many retirement plans is counting on money from your children. Layoffs, rising costs, and other factors may make it impossible for even the best-intentioned children to support their own families and you as well. Therefore, you should not count on your children to support you once you have retired. Besides, they are counting on getting their inheritance when you are gone. I know that's cynical but it's absolutely true!

These are just a few of the most common pitfalls in building your retirement plan. Try to start early and build a plan that can provide you with the income to reach your retirement goals. And remember, don't count too heavily on anyone else, including the government, to support you during retirement. Create a plan that you can control and rely on. That's the only way to Golden Pond.

Chapter 9

Estate Planning: Making Sure Your Survivors Stay on Golden Pond

LET'S GET THIS straight right off the bat. This is **not** a chapter that will enable you to GET TO or even STAY on Golden Pond. After all, for the most part, estate planning is meant to make sure that your affairs are in order after your time on Golden Pond is up, and that your survivors and beneficiaries get to keep most (if not all) of what you accumulated during your lifetime.

The main purpose of estate planning is to pass your assets on to your beneficiaries in the manner you desire (rather than being dictated by State law) and to try to minimize the amount you give to Uncle Sam, your unintended, but notoriously extravagant beneficiary.

Also, keep in mind that this is not a book on estate planning. This is merely a chapter on a topic that could take volumes to complete. The chapter is meant to show you some of the vulnerabilities and misconceptions that most people have when it comes to matters relating to their estates.

Since estate planning deals with the matter of your death (a most decidedly unpleasant circumstance), there is a tendency for most people to want to ignore the subject. They hope the matter will just go away. But, let's face it, folks. **Nobody is going to get out of this world alive!** At some point, we all have to go to the Big Beyond. It is inevitable. The only question is when. Once we accept that reality, the only thing that matters is being prepared for it. Preparation involves taking actions to make sure that you do not leave behind a mess for your survivors and that you minimize (or preferably, eliminate) Uncle Sam's (and your state's) take. These actions, if taken in timely fashion and done correctly, will enable your survivors to get to their own Golden Pond. By taking these actions, you will have removed the biggest barrier to estate planning—the misconception that you are going to live forever, or at least not die for a long, long time, giving you enough time to take care of the matter "some time in the future."

Okay, so now you admit that you will need to do "something." But what are the things you should watch out for? What do you need to get done so that your surviving spouse does not find himself or herself Up The Creek, after perhaps having just spent time on Golden Pond?

In my experience, the biggest barriers to estate planning are:

1. **Thinking you are immortal**, or that you will die when you are finally ready to go.

2. **Feeling that you are "small potatoes,"** and, as such, do not really have an estate to plan for. Keep in mind, though, that under ordinary circumstances, life insurance proceeds do become part of your estate and are subject to taxes. In many cases, a person's net worth may not be large enough to be taxed at the federal level, but with life insurance proceeds added in, estate taxes could be triggered. People have heard that life insurance proceeds are not taxable and so they fail to consider it for estate planning. Yes, insurance proceeds are not subject to income tax but they are subject to estate tax (note that there is a way to bypass the estate tax on life insurance proceeds through the use of Irrevocable Life Insurance Trusts).

3. **Thinking that you do not need a will** because all of your assets are titled as "joint tenancy with right of survivorship" with your beneficiary will eliminate the need for wills and/or estate planning.

4. **Being intimidated by lawyers** and not wanting to appear dumb in front of this professional. As a result, you avoid all contact

with him, in spite of all the benefits that can be derived from this relationship. I concede, the language they use ("legalese") is enough to scare anybody. Just look at how a lawyer would recite The Lord's Prayer. Instead of just saying "Give us this day our daily bread," the lawyer says:

We herby petition, request, and entreat
That due and adequate provision be made
This day and date first above inscribed
For satisfying the petitioners'
Daily nutritional requirements
And for organizing such methods of allocation
To assure prompt and efficient receipt
By and for said petitioners of cereal products
Hereinafter referred to as "bread."

You have to admit, even the Lord would be intimidated by that language. However, you have to remember the lawyer is working for you, and if he is any good, he will try his hardest to make you feel at ease and explain matters to you that may be "over your head."

5. You do not trust lawyers, possibly because you are intimidated by them, and you most certainly do not want to pay "the outrageous fees those crooks charge!" Most often, this is merely an excuse not to do the estate planning that brings you face to face with your own mortality.

Ninety nine percent of lawyers give the rest of them a bad name. (Just joking!)

6. You believe that the new federal exemption limits (Exhibit 9-1) preclude you from paying estate taxes, so you decide against doing any estate tax planning. First of all, the new limits are set to expire (this is called "sunset" in lawyer lingo) in 2011 and revert back to the limits that were in place in 2001. In the past, you could get a credit against the amount you owed on your federal estate tax for the money you paid on the state death tax. Because some states are worried that the potential for an exemption could reduce their collection, some states have rewritten their tax laws so they are no longer tied to the federal rules. In essence, these states have "decoupled" from the federal estate tax, and as a result, some estates, which do not owe any taxes under the federal rules, will end up owing taxes under the new state laws.

7. **You do not have the time.** This, in my opinion, is a classic cop-out. Okay, I grant that some people are so disorganized that it would take some time to collect the data that the attorney might need to prepare your wills or trusts. But just think of the consequences: higher taxes, no guardians named for your minor children, and no specific beneficiaries. Moreover, if you cannot get organized enough to create an estate plan, exactly what kind of a mess are you going to leave behind for your spouse and children? I don't care how busy you are; believe me, you have the time to collect the data. You have to consider it a high priority and just do it.

8. **Reluctance to make decisions.** There are people who just cannot decide who will take care of their minor children, or how they should split up the estate among their beneficiaries. Because of all the relationships and personalities involved, people decide to cross their fingers and leave it to fate. As a consequence, they take no action, and that's the absolute worst thing that someone can do.

I know of a couple that has no children. She has five siblings; he has one. While trying to prepare the will, he wanted to split the assets, allocating 50 percent to his family and 50 percent to hers. This meant that his sibling would get half the estate and her five siblings would split the remaining half. She wanted to split the estate among all of the siblings equally, meaning each sibling would get one-sixth of the estate. She thought he was being unreasonable with his proposal. He thought she was being unreasonable with hers. Fifteen years later, they still cannot decide on how to allocate the money, and the will remains unwritten. If they die simultaneously, state law will dictate how the estate will be divided. If they die separately, the surviving spouse will likely prepare a will based on his or her preference.

9. **Believing that the estate tax will be eliminated.** Under current law, the estate tax is totally eliminated for people who die in

2010. After that, the exemption level reverts to the amount in effect in 2001 ($1 million). However, there is considerable speculation that in the near future, Congress might raise the estate tax exemption to such a high level per decedent (say, $3.5 million), that most people would be exempt from estate taxation.

Regardless of whether the federal estate tax disappears completely, is reduced, or goes back to the way it was in 2001, it would be extremely foolish to ignore the state portion of the estate tax, usually called the State Inheritance Tax. The state will want its fair share.

10. **Unwillingness to pay the lawyer's fees.** Another pitfall is simply that too many people don't want to pay the lawyer's fees to set up any kind of estate plan. They believe that the attorney is going to charge them too much money to help them put together a will or trust. Many people think that an attorney is going to use a boilerplate approach and just fill in a few names and numbers. This is usually not the case. But even if it was, you have to look at it from the viewpoint of the benefit the service provides for you and your beneficiaries. Those names and numbers are of great significance to your beneficiaries, and it is well worth spending the few thousand dollars on their behalf.

Not spending the money would be a big mistake on your part and could work to your detriment. Unfortunately, in the area of personal finance, I often see people unwilling to do something that is obviously in their best interest, only because they are concerned about a professional getting rich at their expense. These people fail to acknowledge the benefits that a professional could provide them. He could be saving his estate hundreds of thousands of dollars in taxes, but he just cannot bring himself to pay the attorney's fees which could run $3,000 to $5,000!

Believe me, the money you are saving can end up costing your beneficiaries a lot of their inheritance, maybe even all of it. I hear people say, "So what if the government gets the money, I didn't have anything when I was born, so why should I leave the money to my kids?" Personally, I think that's a very selfish point of view, and I would prefer not to work with individuals who have this attitude. If you've worked hard to make money and to take care of a family, why not make sure they are taken care of after you are gone? After all, it's more likely that the people you choose to inherit your money will spend it more wisely than the government. Typically, at the root of this problem is the fact that the person spending the money to set up a will or a trust won't be around to benefit from it. After all, when the benefits of the work performed by the attorney are finally realized, you're no longer around.

People have to wrestle with the idea of their own mortality to begin with. Then they have to spend money to address the issue, making them even more reluctant and uncomfortable. Many people therefore simply avoid it.

The barriers mentioned above lead to vulnerabilities such as:

A. Not having a will

It never ceases to amaze me how many people out there do not even have a basic will that will indicate what they want done with their money, and more importantly, **who will take care of their minor children and how**. The designation of guardians in your will is not binding on the court, but it is very persuasive.

I know of one incident where a young couple died in an accident while on a vacation, leaving behind three very young children. They died without a will, and an endless war broke out between the two sets of grandparents as to who would get custody of the children and who would get the money. Remember, if you do not specify your wishes in a will, your assets might be handled according to state laws in a manner that would just not have been what you wanted. At the very least, as in the case of the three children, costly and long-drawn out court battles, with lots of bitterness can result, harming the very people you were trying to protect.

While you may not want to think about it, if you want to leave the assets which you have worked so hard to earn to your loved ones, you'll need to take the time to put together a will. If you die without a will ("intestate"), state law would dictate how your estate gets split up among your family at death.

I also know of a situation where a young physician died suddenly. He had not prepared a will, so his estate was divided into 50 percent for his wife and 50 percent for his two minor children. The children's portion was put into a trust, to be distributed when the children reached the age of twenty-one. In the meantime, his widow had to support the children from her portion of the estate. Her share was so depleted by the time the children were twenty-one that she had to go back to work. In the meantime, her children were millionaires by the time they had graduated from college! I am sure that this was not what the husband intended. **Exhibit 9-2** lists the various advantages of having a will.

One of the reasons people don't do proper estate planning or even make a will is that they don't believe they have an estate. People will typically say: "No, I don't have that kind of money...I don't have an estate." In reality, an estate is not just the accumulated wealth of the rich; the possessions of even an average individual could be considered as "estate." Any assets that you have accumulated are considered part of your estate, **including the money from an insurance policy**. Believe me, you do not have to be super-wealthy to have an "estate." If you pay off your mortgage, save for Golden Pond, have life insurance, and inherit from your parents, you could easily get over the exemption amount.

Another reason people avoid making a will is because they are concerned that, in addition to the time involved, it will be a difficult process that they won't understand. The process typically involves organizing what you have and making some key decisions, most of which can be reviewed and updated. You should list your assets and determine how you want them distributed in a tax-effective manner to your beneficiaries.

When orchestrating your will, there are two key decisions you will need to make: 1. naming an executor who will oversees the distribution of assets; and 2. if you have children who are still minors, you will need to determine who their guardians will be.

If for no other reason, this last reason is an impetus for many people to make a will, simply to make sure their children are raised by guardians of their choice and not those appointed by the state, who might not be the people you would select to raise your children.

B. Not Updating Your Will

The other common pitfall that many people run into is that once they have finally agreed to prepare a will, they lock it away and never update it. This can result in an ex-spouse receiving some of your assets instead of the grieving widow. When children are born, when someone remarries, or when a beneficiary or the executor passes away, you need to update your will. **Sometimes it's even harder to get someone to go back and update a will than it is to coax them to finally prepare one in the first place**. A will that has not been updated to include the people who are now in your life may be worse than having no will at all. You may be leaving your estate to the wrong people. Therefore, you need to make the necessary changes to your will, in conjunction with changes in your life. Once you've done this, sign it and destroy the old will.

In addition to a will, you should have a **living will**. This is a document that allows you to specify which life-prolonging measures you do, and do not, want to be taken in the event that you become terminally ill or incapacitated. Also, a **durable power of attorney** for health care and for property is an essential component of your estate plan. This authorizes the person you designate to act on your behalf if you were to become incapacitated.

C. Not having a trust.

There are two types of trusts—those that are created while you are alive ("living"), and those that are created on your death ("testamentary"). Living trusts, as the name indicates, are created while you are alive and there are two types of these: revocable and irrevocable. The conditions of the revocable living trust can be changed by you at any time and the assets are under your control at all times. On the other hand, an irrevocable trust is not in your control and the conditions of the trust can never be changed. The assets within the irrevocable trust pass on to the next generation and the growth of the assets within the trust are not subject to estate taxes, and also offer protection against lawsuits. An irrevocable life insurance trust is an excellent device that allows you to bypass the estate taxation of the proceeds on your life insurance policy.

Testamentary trusts are created on your death. An example of testamentary trusts is the "spousal trust" (also called the "A" trust), which utilizes the unlimited marital deduction to bypass estate taxation of assets left to the surviving spouse and the credit shelter trust" (also called the "B" trust), which utilizes the exemption amount of the decedent for assets left to individuals other than the spouse (e.g. children.). The surviving spouse has the right to withdraw 5 percent of the principal on an annual basis, as well as the yearly earnings (interest and dividends) from the trust. The surviving spouse, however, does not have the right to change the beneficiaries of the "B" trust. This is an excellent mechanism by which a spouse can make sure that the rights of the children are protected in case the surviving spouse decides to remarry.

It should be obvious by now that you really should consult with an attorney on the matter of estate planning. Please do not try this at home by yourself. This is not a do-it-yourself project. The stakes are just too high, and there is no room for error! Since most of the documents only go into effect at your death, it might be a bit too late to correct any errors you may have made. Moreover, you could be leaving a big mess for your loved ones.

Not everyone needs to set up a trust. However, if you have a significant amount of assets in your estate you may want to have a trust or a living trust to help you control the distribution and management of your assets. A trust can help your beneficiaries avoid probate, which often means waiting as long as two years before your property can be transferred to your beneficiaries. Also, since probate is a court hearing, the records are open to the public, whereas a trust is a personal document, which is not open to the public, allowing you to keep personal matters between members of the family.

The average cost of probate is usually 10 percent of the gross estate and involves fees paid to the attorney, the executor, the inheritance tax referee, and compensation for other officers of the court. Also, other related probate fees must be paid before any of the decedent's estate can be paid to the beneficiaries.

A trust can provide ease of administration and guidance for the beneficiaries, especially if the children are coming into a lot of money through the inheritance. A trust can serve as a means of guiding individuals who may otherwise not be familiar with handling such large sums of money. You really do not want your twenty-two-year-old son to get control of several hundred thousand dollars, do you? It should also be noted that despite common misconceptions, **trusts do not help you avoid paying taxes. Exhibit 9-3** lists the various advantages of having a trust.

D. Failure to organize

One of the most important aspects of estate planning is organization. Out of concerns for your beneficiaries, you should have a listing of where important documents are kept. Too often beneficiaries are left in the dark. Whether it is a will, bank account information, brokerage statements, or insurance policies, and in this high-tech world we live in, **even usernames and passwords**, someone needs to be able to find important documents. The key to a safety deposit box, the deed to a home, or the ownership papers for a car or boat all need to be accessible to someone. I recommend that you keep such important materials in one location and keep the original copy of the will out of the safety deposit box to assure that someone can gain access to it.

People are often fearful of letting others know where such important documents are. They don't want to worry children with such details and are mistrusting of others. Unfortunately, it is not uncommon for heirs to have a very difficult time organizing and handling the estate of someone because the necessary documents are not organized, or worse, they cannot be located The simple act of organizing key documents can be extremely helpful in estate planning and could be a time saver and, consequently, a cost saver.

E. Not taking full advantage of estate tax laws.

There are two tax breaks available to any individual: **unlimited marital deduction (UMD) and an exemption amount.** Each decedent can leave his or her surviving spouse any amount, without fear of having to pay estate taxes on the amount. Each decedent also gets an exemption of $2 million (for 2006-2008) for amounts left to people other than their spouses, making the total exemption amount $4 million (for 2006-2008) per couple.

Sometimes through lack of planning, people leave everything to their surviving spouse, thereby taking advantage of the UMD. That's fine, as long as the surviving spouse's resulting estate is less than the exemption amount ($2 million for 2006-2008) and is expected to remain below the exemption amount (see **Table 9-1** for future exemption amounts) for his or her lifetime. But if the resulting estate will exceed the exemption amount, then the surviving spouse's estate may wind up paying estate taxes that may have been eliminated or at least reduced to a significant degree. Under current laws, no one pays estate taxes if their estate is less than $2 million. With proper planning, both spouses can use their exemptions, thereby saving taxes on the additional $2 million—a potential savings of $780,800 in federal estate taxes (see **Exhibit 9-1**).

F. Not Understanding the problems with joint tenancy

People have the misconception that if they have joint tenancy with right of survivorship that they don't need to do anything else, much less have a will. **If, however, you have a sizable estate, joint tenancy could be the worst thing you could do**. The current limit is $2 million dollars that can pass through joint tenancy from one spouse to the other without estate taxes. As per **Exhibit 9-1**, this will increase in the year 2009 to $3.5 million.

Titling all your assets as 'joint tenancy with right of survivorship" (JTWROS) is the same as over-utilizing the UMD and under-utilizing the exemption amount. This could result in estate taxes that could quite possibly have been totally avoided.

In 2006, if the husband dies with an estate of, say, $3 million, and the wife has $1 million dollars, then through joint tenancy everything will go to the wife and her estate will be worth $4 million. Since her exemption is at $2 million dollars, she will then pay estate taxes on the excess $2 million. In this scenario, the husband utilized the UMD to such an extent that he did not take any advantage of his own exemption of $2 million, which is allowed to **each** decedent. He wasted the exemption amount he was entitled to by relying solely on the UMD. With better planning, federal estate taxation could have been avoided on the entire $4 million. As mentioned previously, the additional $2 million in the estate of the surviving spouse has the potential to increase taxes by as much as $780,800 (as shown in **Exhibit 9-1**).

Other problems with joint tenancy stem from the fact that assets are held jointly, and this may create problems when decisions need to be made about what happens to the property or assets at the death of the surviving spouse. Since two people are involved, changes are more difficult to make than when updating a will. Problems can also arise regarding how the money will be handled by the remaining spouse in regard to children and other heirs. Joint tenancy does not account for leaving money to the children, but puts the assets or property in the hands solely of the remaining spouse. Additionally, if the property or assets have a lien against them or there are debts to be paid, these are also transferred to the remaining spouse. The creation and utilization of trusts would be extremely beneficial in these cases. There is also a common misconception that joint tenancy replaces the need for a will. This is not true, as properties not owned as joint tenants need to be included in a will.

JTWROS should only be used between married individuals. The pitfalls of JTWROS with someone other than your spouse could be that the assets become exposed to the creditors of your joint owner, or you could create gift tax consequences. Also, probate is required when the surviving joint tenant dies. And something that most people do not consider : if one joint tenant becomes incapacitated and unable to act, the other must go to court and become appointed as "conservator" before being able to do anything with the jointly owned assets. Usually, an inheritor of an asset gets a "step up" in basis on the death of the decedent.

That is, the inheritor's cost basis becomes the value of the asset on the date of death (or six months after that date.) The "step up" allows an inheritor to avoid the capital gains tax on the appreciation of the asset since the original date of purchase by the decedent. When you utilize joint tenancy in any form, from an income tax viewpoint, the death of one joint tenant permits a stepped-up cost basis on only one half of the jointly owned property. **This is why Joint Tenancy is never a good option in most cases - it destroys the ability to plan and reduce estate taxes.** The solution to the problem? Consider the use of trusts.

G. Not understanding estate planning

It is not uncommon to find people who are simply **afraid of looking foolish in front of an attorney**. They don't understand estate planning, and they don't want to appear ignorant, so they avoid the issue. It's true that a lot of estate planning is wrapped up in legal mumbo jumbo and the material can be quite tedious to read. However, it is important to take some time and learn the basics. Get an idea of what wills and trusts are all about. Learn about the different options you have in regard to providing money for your family and your beneficiaries without giving the government the largest chunk. There are plenty of books, web sites, and even seminars available to help you gain a basic education about estate planning. **By becoming more informed, you won't be turning an attorney loose with a blank check.**

It is also to your advantage to hire a good quarterback, someone who will be your financial advisor and lead you through the various options. There is nothing wrong with asking for help, and letting it be known that you don't know a lot about estate planning. You're not alone. Most people know very little about the topic and for that reason, experts can be valuable. Find someone with whom you feel comfortable, and let them guide you through the process.

H. Not changing the title to your assets to conform to trusts

One of the most common mistakes we see in estate planning is that people will spend thousands of dollars to prepare a very elaborate estate plan. They will dutifully sign all the documents and then commit one of the biggest blunders in personal finance: **they forget to change the title of their assets to conform to the conditions and details of their estate planning documents!**

For example, they might develop revocable living trusts to take optimal advantage of the UMD and the exemption amount (currently $2 million per individual). But they forget about the time it takes to re-title their assets from individual or joint tenancy to the respective revocable trust. By neglecting to do that, they have negated all of the tax benefits of having trusts in the first place. Remember, **if you take the time to re-title your assets while you are alive, you won't have to pay a judge to do it after you're dead.**

J. Not keeping up-to-date with changes

This is similar to what was discussed in Pitfall #2 in this chapter, but this pertains more to **external** changes (e.g. estate and income tax laws) that could have a direct bearing on the estate plan you may already have created, or are planning to create.

Keep in mind that estate planning is a journey, not a destination. In other words, the most important part of your estate planning is keeping your documents current with changes in your personal life as well as tax laws so that they will do what you intend them to do at the appropriate time. From the day you have your documents prepared until the day you die, you will probably need to amend your documents several times, adding or removing beneficiaries, changing the distribution of your assets, changing executors, and adapting to changes in tax laws and personal circumstances. To prevent your documents from becoming outdated and obsolete, and for maximum effectiveness, you will have to review them periodically and update them as necessary.

In summary, don't fall victim to these or other pitfalls. Take the time to organize and get your affairs in order with the help of a professional. The time and money you spend will benefit those closest to you and ease the transition of your loved survivors to their own Golden Pond.

Exhibit 9-1
Estate Tax Exclusion

Year	Exclusion	Credit
2006 – 2008	$2,000,000	$780,800
2009	$3,500,000	$1,455,800
2010	No Tax	No Tax
Past Years		
1986 – 1997	$600,000	$192,800
1998	$625,000	$202,050
1999	$650,000	$211,300
2000 – 2001	$675,000	$220,550
2002 – 2003	$1,000,000	$345,800
2004 – 2005	$1,500,000	$555,800

Exhibit 9-2
Advantages of Having a Will

- A will can say where your property goes at death. If you die without a will, the courts will declare that you died "intestate" and your property will be distributed based on state law. This may result in a distribution contrary to your wishes. A will allows you to specify where your property goes at your death and avoids potentially costly disputes between beneficiaries after your death.

- A will allows you to place conditions on the distribution. If you died intestate, you could place a small fortune in the hands of an eighteen-year-old child with no strings attached. A will allows you to leave a gift in trust for the benefit of your child, paying out the income from the trust, but withholding the principal until your child reaches a responsible age.

- A will allows you to minimize estate taxes. Federal and state estate tax rates can be much higher than income tax rates. A will can minimize estate tax exposure, by ensuring maximum use of each spouse's individual exemption from estate taxes, through a built-in device called a "credit shelter trust."

- A will can name the person to act as your Executor. The Executor is the person who accumulates all of you assets, pays off any liabilities, and distributes the remainder of your estate to your beneficiaries. State law requires an executor to post a bond to protect against the loss of estate funds resulting from negligence or fraud by the executor. A will can eliminate the need for an executor to transact with a bonding or insurance company.

- A will can name a guardian for your minor children. Although not binding, this is a very persuasive way to document your wishes.

- A will can spell out how your estate is managed. By specifically authorizing the executor to engage in certain basic transactions, a will can spare the executor from having to have those transactions approved by the court.

- A will can minimize the time your estate spends in probate court. Probate is a protracted, costly, and public process. Your estate would probably need to hire an attorney to manage the process. Furthermore, while your estate goes through probate, anyone can go to the courthouse and find out the value of the estate, the individual assets, and the names of the beneficiaries. A will can ensure efficient probate administration. Only assets titled in your name, without a beneficiary designation, are subject to probate. Most assets can be titled in the name of a trust to avoid the probate process, as discussed in Exhibit 9-3.

Exhibit 9-3
Advantages of Having a Trust

- A trust allows you to avoid probate entirely. By transferring assets into a trust during your lifetime, there is no need to submit them to the probate court to change the legal title upon your death. This saves considerable time and expense. The advantage is magnified if there is real property in another state, which would require an ancillary probate proceeding. The main disadvantage of trusts is that they require you to re-title and transfer assets to the trust during your lifetime, to ensure they pass outside of probate.

- A trust keeps your assets private. Since there is no need to report assets to the probate court, they do not get entered on the public record.

- A trust allows a trustee to manage your assets if you become incapacitated. Without a trust, a financial power of attorney would have to be executed, or the court would have to appoint a guardian to manage your assets on your behalf.

Chapter 10

Getting Professional Help

OKAY, BY NOW you have hopefully developed some idea of what it would take to reach your own Golden Pond. It might appear to be a daunting task. But, to paraphrase a popular saying, **it doesn't matter how long the journey is, it is more important that you take the first step.**

Financial planning is just like starting your own exercise program. The goal might seem far away at the beginning, but once you get started, it gets easier with each day you actually do it. The important thing is to work on it regularly and set aside some time for it. Yes, it will take time and effort, but the rewards are well worth it.

But, let's get one thing straight. If you have the time, the expertise, and the inclination to research and study the various aspects of putting together a retirement plan, you are your own best advisor. **After all, no one is more interested in your own financial well-being than you are.** There is plenty of financial information readily available right at your fingertips. And with computers available at a fraction of what they used to cost as little as five years ago, you could easily become adept at preparing your own retirement plan. You can learn the basics of constructing a retirement plan and working within your own comfort zone, and then put together a plan for your future. This will cost you nothing except your own time.

However, in this fast-paced, sound bite-oriented world we live in, most people do not have the time to prepare the plan or to develop the expertise. Nor do they have the inclination or the persistence necessary to study all of the details involved in building a solid retirement plan. Sometimes they may lack the discipline and focus to follow through on their plan's development and implementation. Some may never develop the expertise to identify and address the various vulnerabilities that could prevent them from reaching Golden Pond.

And, most commonly, **some people realize that they just do not have enough confidence in their ability.** They do not have enough confidence in the plan they have produced for themselves, and, therefore, they never take the steps necessary to implement the plan.

Plus, they might have misunderstood some technical points on the way to developing their own plan which could have the potential of making their way to Golden Pond much more difficult. There are others who may possess the expertise and the time to do their own planning and money management but would prefer to delegate the responsibility to a trusted advisor while they enjoy the finer things in life and pursue the things they feel more passionate about.

If you believe this pretty much describes your situation, you probably know that you need professional help. Just like you would hire a personal trainer to get you going in the right direction on an exercise program, you need to hire a professional to help you avoid mistakes, to keep you on track, and ultimately, to make sure you succeed in reaching your goals.

After almost a quarter of a century in the financial advisory business, I suppose I am biased. But I truly believe **everyone needs professional help**—whether they have the time, the inclination, or the expertise. Some might need more professional help than others. Even if you have prepared a good plan all by yourself, it would behoove you to at least get it reviewed by a professional.

Why do you need professional help? Because **the possibility of making mistakes is too great, and the cost of making mistakes even greater.** You just do not want to find out too late that due to some incorrect calculations, invalid assumptions, or basic misunderstanding of some vital concept you are Up The Creek, instead of On Golden Pond. Worse yet, some of these errors could have ramifications even after you after your death and beyond; they may also affect your survivors and beneficiaries! There is a saying: "A person who acts as his own lawyer has a fool for a client." It's especially true in this case. You want to make sure you have not overlooked anything. Therefore, you need to place your trust in a qualified professional—a financial advisor who is available to act as your coach or personal trainer. The question then becomes, **how does one find such an expert in whom they can place their trust?** After all, the newspapers are full of stories about con artists who posed as financial advisors and ripped off little old ladies of all of their life savings. The problem is compounded by the fact that there are really very few barriers to entry in this young profession. A person could hang up a shingle and call himself a financial advisor and a lay person would have no way of knowing the advisor's level of competency until it was too late. Every profession has its share of charlatans and crooks. And even though the vast, overwhelming majority of financial advisors are capable, honest, and caring, you still want to minimize the possibility of winding up with a charlatan who is unethical, unscrupulous, or just plain incompetent.

What does the advisor do?

Before we begin the search for a competent professional to help you get to Golden Pond, let us determine what you need from that professional.

A good financial advisor helps you make smart choices about your money. To be able to do so, he should work on creating a retirement plan for you based on your own unique circumstances: your age, your work situation, your assets and liabilities, your level of risk tolerance and, of course, your specific retirement goals and objectives. He should be able to point out your current vulnerabilities and recommend steps to reduce or eliminate them. He should be able to develop an investment strategy that blends your risk tolerance and your objectives and then, perhaps, monitor your progress towards Golden Pond. He should be able and available to answer your questions and concerns. He should be able to help you avoid making financial mistakes that could prove hazardous to your wealth and affect your ability to retire in the manner in which you would like to become accustomed. If you hire him to also manage your assets, you have to make sure he has the knowledge and the expertise to do so. Remember, he is your confidante and you have to have full faith, trust, and confidence in him. In a sense, he is perhaps even the quarterback of your financial team (which includes the attorney, the insurance agent, the tax preparer, and the stock broker,), while you serve as the general manager. **Exhibit 10-1** is a comprehensive list of the duties and responsibilities of a financial advisor.

I know it's confusing, but the terms "financial advisor" and "investment advisor" are often used interchangeably. For registration and licensing, even the Securities & Exchange Commission (SEC) calls these professionals "Registered Investment Advisers" (RIA and, yes, they do spell advisor with an "e"). For the purposes of this book, and especially this chapter, these terms are interchangeable.

An article by TD Waterhouse (now TD Ameritrade) entitled "What You Need To Know About Financial Advice," explains that in the financial world today, there are basically two types of advice available to investors: through brokerage relationships, and through advisory relationships (fee or commission- based). There is a huge difference between the two. Unfortunately, the person on the street usually is totally unaware of the difference between these two types of advice, or that a difference even exists. Among other things, the article talks about the difference between investment advisors and stockbrokers and the advantages of working with the former over the latter. As per the article, here are some of the key differences and advantages:

Investment advisors have a fiduciary duty to act in the best interests of their clients at all times. Brokerage firms generally are not fiduciaries to their customers and therefore do not make decisions that are based solely in their customers' best interests.

Investment advisors provide their clients with a Form ADV that describes exactly how the investment advisor does business, his background and qualifications, and obtains the client's consent to any conflicts of interest that do exist in his business. Brokerage firms are not required to provide any comparable type of disclosure.

Financial advisors charge clients a fee negotiated in advance and cannot earn any other profits from their clients without the client's prior consent. Most advisors charge a fee based on a percentage of the assets under management, so there is no potential for conflict of interest. A stockbroker's income could increase even if the customer's portfolio went down in value.

Financial advisors manage money in the best interest of their clients and are not involved in other business activities like investment banking and underwriting, which brokerage firms do. These other businesses could represent a conflict of interest and may cause the brokerage firm's interest or attention to focus on other areas of the firm outside of their retail brokerage business and customers.

In addition to what the article says, there are some other differences as well. Investment advisors are required to maintain their registration by undergoing a certain amount of continuing education. This enables the advisor to keep up with the state of the art. No such education requirement exists in the brokerage industry.

Usually, investment advisors possess a more well-rounded background, allowing them to offer advice on a wide variety of personal financial matters such as income taxes, insurance, estate, cash flow, and budgeting. Stockbrokers typically have a much narrower focus, usually just investments.

Most importantly, investment advisors are **independent**. As such, they are better able to provide **objective** advice, products, and services. Usually, the stockbroker has to say and do exactly what has been dictated to from upper management. He cannot offer a stock that has not been approved by the firm and he cannot send out any material that has not been approved. Sometimes he may find that the customer's bottom line and his firm's bottom line are at odds with each other. And, I'll give you one guess as to which he will be forced to choose.

Look once again at **Exhibit 10-1**. These are the functions of an investment advisor. Now check off the ones performed by a stockbroker. Do you see the difference? An investment advisor is, first and foremost, a fiduciary—a legal term suggesting that the advisor is held to a higher ethical standard than a stockbroker

I don't know whether you caught this in the preceding paragraphs, but I should point out that users of investment advisory services are referred to as **clients**, while users of brokerage services are referred to as **customers.** I do not know whether Waterhouse intended to create that distinction, but as far as I am concerned, that subtle difference says it all.

Where to find advisors

Just where do you find a competent professional to trust and put your faith in? There are many professional organizations that refer their members to the general public. Three of the most respected and highly accredited organizations in the financial field are the Financial Planning Association (FPA), the National Association of Personal Financial Advisors (NAPFA), and the American Institute of Certified Public Accountants' Personal Finance Specialist (AICPA/PFS) division. These organizations can provide you with information about planners and a means of finding one in your area. To be sure, there are other organizations with members that provide similar services and those can be researched on the Internet. These three, however, are the ones that I am most familiar with.

FPA

The Financial Planning Association, which can be reached at 800-647-6340 (www.fpanet.org), is the membership organization for the financial planning community that provides information and literature about financial topics to consumers. Certified Financial Planners (CFP®'s) as well as accountants, bankers, and other financial professionals are members of the FPA. Available through the association is the FPA's Planner Search, which allows individuals to seek qualified CFP® practitioners in their area.

NAPFA

The National Association of Personal Financial Advisors, which can be reached at 800-366-2732 (www.napfa.org), provides brochures, both on and off line, that help in the process of selecting a personal advisor. The twenty-one-year-old organization of fee-only planners includes members from all over the country who operate under a strict code of ethics. There are also advisors available on the web site to answer specific financial questions.

AICPA

The Personal Finance Specialist (PFS) designation is a subset of the American Institute of Certified Public Accountants and can be contacted at 800-708-8775 (www.pfp.aicpa.org). While the members are just as qualified as the other two organizations mentioned above, it does suffer from a lack of marketing and, therefore, a lack of awareness on the part of the general public. While a financial advisor could become a CFP with a minimum of educational background (most do have at least an undergraduate degree in liberal arts or the sciences), the PFS designees has to be a Certified Public Accountant (CPA) to belong to this group. Some consumers therefore, get some comfort knowing that the advisor has some educational credentials to back up his shingle.

As I already mentioned, there are other organizations and associations offering other designations that could help you locate an advisor in your area. However, in my opinion, the three organizations mentioned above should be more than enough to get you started.

Okay, once you have a list of advisors, you have to narrow it down to three or so that most fit your needs. Some you can eliminate based on geography; their offices might be at a distance that is considerably greater than what you are willing to travel. Although this might be an initial consideration, over time, distance takes on lesser and lesser significance. **While distance may be a consideration, you do not want to eliminate a perfectly competent professional based on that criterion alone**. We have clients who started with us in Chicago, and then retired to places as far away as Montana, upstate New York, Las Vegas, California, and even Singapore. Like I said, distance begins to matter less and less once the trust and rapport is established.

To narrow the list further, you might wish to consider **"The 4 E's:"**

1. Education

You want to know the advisor's **educational background**, especially as it relates to finance. A broad educational background is preferable, with perhaps even a graduate degree thrown in for good measure. Besides just college education, you have to find out how he manages to keep abreast of the constant changes in tax laws, market conditions, etc. How many hours does he devote to **continuing professional education**?

2. Experience

This criterion is even more important than education. You want someone who has had a broad-based experience that would enable him to provide on-going all-around consulting help to you. Has he seen and done enough to be able to help you - has he experienced bear and bull markets? What kind of experience did he have prior to being a financial advisor? You definitely do not want someone who happened to have been laid off from his job as, say, an engineer and who decided to start his own financial planning practice because he could not get a job in his regular profession. Not that it's wrong to start fresh in a new profession; you just want to make sure that he is serious about it, is committed to it, and that he will not abandon his new vocation (and you) as soon as he gets another job in his original field of expertise.

I have seen annuities and life insurance being sold by cab drivers and limousine chauffeurs to their passengers. How can the driver expect to be treated as a professional under those circumstances? And even if someone did decide to purchase one of those products from him, what assurance does the customer have that the product vendor (that's what he is!) will still be in the profession to answer any questions he may have in the future?

3. Ethics

Then there is the question of ethics. This is perhaps the toughest criterion to evaluate. **Usually you cannot tell if the advisor is ethical until it is probably too late.** However, you can take certain steps to minimize or even eliminate that possibility. It is great if you can find an advisor through a referral by a friend or relative who has worked with that professional. If you don't have any such person to ask for referrals, you have to ask the professional for references, **and then take the time to contact those references.** Granted that these references may be only names of the advisor's best clients, but talk to them and ask them questions pertaining to matters that are of importance to you. Ask them about their experiences with the advisor. Don't concern yourself as much with the performance of the portfolio as with the character and experience of the advisor.

When I ask for a show of hands at my seminars for the attendees' retirement objectives, NOT ONE PERSON has ever said that their goal in life was to "beat the S&P 500." You want to know if the advisor understands **your** specific needs and builds a plan around **your** goals and objectives. Remember, you do not want to hire a salesperson who is pushing products like insurance, annuities, or mutual funds just to generate commissions for himself.

4. Empathy

"People don't care how much you know until they know how much you care." This is so true when it comes to choosing an advisor and perhaps is one of the most desirable qualities you should seek in the advisor. He **has** to care about you and what you are trying to accomplish. He has to place your interests before his own. You can usually determine the empathy first of all by talking to the advisor. Does he ask lots of questions and then take the time to really listen to your answers? Does he answer phone calls promptly?

Along with the 4 E's, one other important criterion is rapport. How do you get along with the advisor? Is there any chemistry between you? Do you like and respect each other? If you answer "no" to any of these, the relationship is destined to fail. Remember, this is not like going to H&R Block to get your income tax return prepared once a year. In most cases, **it is a "cradle to grave" relationship**, and the person you hire or have hired is going to be your trusted family advisor, hopefully over a long, long time— perhaps even for life. If you feel uneasy or intimidated by him, if he appears to be condescending, if he appears to be too busy to talk with you every time you call—all of these are warning signs about the quality of the relationship. There is no question about it; you have to genuinely like each other and feel comfortable with each other or it isn't going to work. It's as simple as that.

Registration

You have to find out if the advisor is duly licensed and registered. Advisors are regulated by the Securities & Exchange Commission (SEC) if they manage more than $25 million in client assets. If they manage less than that, they are subject to their respective state regulation. When you first meet with an advisor, he is required to provide you with a Disclosure Document (Form ADV, Part II) that describes in detail his qualifications and background, as well as details regarding his method of compensation. Look it over very carefully and ask questions if you do not understand something. Be Selective

There is nothing wrong with meeting several financial advisors before you decide with whom you wish to work. In fact, it's to your advantage to meet at least two or three. Ask lots of questions. You do not have to feel embarrassed or intimidated. After all, he is going to be working for you. In essence, you're his employer. If he does not want to answer your questions, you can refuse to hire him, and simply find someone else who is more forthcoming.

Among the questions you should ask:

1. What is your educational background? Do you have a degree in finance?

2. How long have you been a financial advisor?

3. How do you keep up with changes in the tax laws, the economy, and the stock market? How many hours in a year do you spend on continuing professional education?

4. Is there a minimum amount of assets a client must have for you to work with them?

5. How are you compensated? If you are fee based, then how are the fees calculated? If you are commission based, then how are the commission calculated? If it is a combination of both, then exactly how does that work?

6. Do you have a contract that spells out your means of compensation?

7. Do you receive any type of financial incentive for selling products from any specific company? Do you deal in proprietary (in-house) products?

8. Can you provide me with at least three references from your list of clients?

9. Will you be able to refer me to an attorney or another professional, if and when it becomes necessary?

10. Will I be working with you or will an associate handle my account?

11. How often do you monitor my account?

12. How will you develop a financial plan for my situation and select appropriate investment vehicles?

13. Do you require my authorization for trading in my portfolio account, or do you manage my portfolio on a "discretionary" basis?

14. Do you provide a comprehensive written analysis of my financial situation and offer recommendations?

15. How often will we meet to update my plan or to review my portfolio? How promptly can I expect you to return my phone calls?

From the answers you receive, your goal is to determine if the advisor is someone who can help assess your needs and build a financial plan that is right for you. It's important that you feel comfortable with the advisor and have confidence that he understands your risk tolerance and your goals, objectives, and even dreams for the future.

Too many people assume that all financial advisors are alike when, in reality, they vary diversely in terms of the 4 E's mentioned above. You do not have to accept their recommendations, especially if they are of the "cookie-cutter" type. And definitely you do not have to accept recommendations that are being shoved down your throat or ones that make you uneasy and uncomfortable. In fact, if the advisor does come up with suggestions that make you feel that way, it means that he may not have been paying close attention to what you were telling him during the interview process. Remember, he is working for **you**, not the other way around. It's your money and your Golden Pond that's at stake here, so act accordingly.

Compensation

This is an area that is subject to so much controversy that it is advisable to go a bit more into details. There are **three primary means of compensation** for financial planners. You should know from the outset in which manner your advisor will be compensated. Many financial advisors work on a commission basis, meaning they receive a commission based on the sale of financial products. Others work on a fee basis. This means they charge either a flat fee or an hourly rate. In a flat fee situation, you typically pay a pre-determined fee while hourly fees are based on an agreed hourly rate, similar to how you pay an attorney for his time.

Financial advisors may also work on a **combined commission and fee** basis. In such cases, the advisor receives an hourly rate or a fixed fee for the time spent on preparing a plan or for consultation, and then receives a commission on financial products sold to the client. Sometimes you will hear the term "fee-offset," which means that the fees charged would be offset by the commissions generated. There are also advisors who consider themselves "fee only," which means that the advisor is never compensated by commissions, as opposed to some "fee-based" advisors who may have some compensation (however negligible) from commissions. Some advisors may charge a set fee or an hourly fee for the plan preparation and then charge an annual fee (typically, 1 percent) based on the client assets managed by the advisor.

One of the most controversial issues in the financial advisory services is which method is supposedly the best. Professionals who are "fee only" consider their method of compensation to be the purest and best, while fee-based or commission-based professionals consider their method of compensation to be the fairest.

In my opinion, it really does not matter how a professional is compensated as long as the client has received full and complete disclosure of method and amount of compensation. Again, in my opinion, just because an advisor is compensated in a certain way does not make him any more competent, more ethical, or more morally superior than a professional who is compensated in a different manner. In my own experience, however, I have found that **fee-based or fee-only advisors are looked upon as more professional, and their recommendations are more readily accepted by clients** than their commission-based brethren who, rightly or wrongly, are considered more like product pushers with inherent conflicts of interest.

There is no hard and fast rule as to which type of compensation is best for your purposes. In fact, throughout the financial industry the fee versus commission debate rages on with no end in sight. What is most important for your purposes is that you understand up front exactly how your advisor will be compensated. Again, ask plenty of questions and make sure you understand the method of compensation before you sign the "Agreement" and start the advisor-client relationship.

Expectations

Here are some basic expectations that you should have of any financial advisor.

He or she:

Must comply with federal and state laws and regulations. Must provide full disclosure about products and services offered. Must update you on the status of your account. Should always be providing you with accurate information and looking out for your best interests. Must hold your financial information in the strictest of confidence at all times. Must disclose all forms of compensation. Should be reachable and return calls or e-mails quickly. Should plan to assess your level of risk early in the process.

In addition, you want to feel that the person with whom you are working is mature enough to handle your finances professionally and confidentially. You should also have a plan for periodic follow up meetings and an ongoing exchange of information. Remember, this is not like going to your local tax preparer who you visit once a year and don't see him again till the following year. As mentioned above, this is a cradle-to-grave type of a relationship, so you have to make absolutely sure that the professional you hire is the one with whom you feel most comfortable. If it's not the right person, then don't hesitate to pull the plug.

Preparation

Not only must the financial advisor meet certain requirements, but for you to work successfully with such an advisor, you too must accept a sense of responsibility in the relationship. If you come in unprepared or do not fully explain your current financial picture or future goals, the advisor cannot do his job adequately.

What are your responsibilities?

Don't hide anything. Provide a complete picture of your financial picture, including your assets, sources of income, investments, insurance, and any outstanding debt. Full disclosure allows an advisor to do his job. Explain what you're trying to do and why you're trying to do it. Make sure he knows your goals and what you are looking to accomplish financially. To do this, you will first need to establish realistic goals. Return his calls promptly. If the advisor is working to help you, don't ignore him when he has questions or recommendations for you. Have your paperwork in order. Besides explaining your financial picture, you should have the necessary papers ready to show your advisor. This includes your last tax return, pay stubs, a list of your income sources, a list of your current expenses, a list of your investments, and a listing of any outstanding debt. All of your financial details should be on paper so that your advisor can use the data to construct a plan. Once you are satisfied that you have found someone with whom you are comfortable, establish a schedule. Plan to have your financial materials together and ready for your next meeting. Meet the advisor when you have a clear head and are not in a rush to get to another appointment. Make your meetings worthwhile. Ask questions. If you don't understand his advice, then ask for a more detailed explanation. If he requests a meeting, there is usually a very good reason for it. So don't ignore such requests. If it is inconvenient, meet with him when it is convenient for you. It's your finances and future at stake here so surely you can set aside some time for it. Remember, he is not calling for the meeting because he does not have anything to do and is looking for a way to pass time.

Remember, you do not have to follow everything he tells you to do. However, if you are hiring someone for their expertise, so why not utilize it? Again, this goes back to feeling comfortable with the person you have selected.

Down the road

Once you have been working with an advisor, and he has presented you with a plan, you will need to review it carefully and ask yourself several questions. For example: Does the plan reflect your level of risk and tolerance? Are there clear recommendations based on your goals and needs? Has the advisor worked within the specific financial constraints you have provided or is she recommending that you make investments that do not meet your needs? Can he elaborate upon, clarify, and explain the reasoning behind all recommendations? Are there provisions for cash, liquidity and emergency funds?

While you're in the process of selecting a financial advisor, you might look for articles on the subject in *Money Magazine*, *Smart Money* or the *Wall Street Journal*. However, while educating yourself on how to find an advisor is important, so is your gut feeling about the person. You'll find advisors who boast about making 50 percent or more returns for their clients. If that is the case, you'll probably wonder why the advisor is working for a living. Shouldn't he or she be off on an exotic island somewhere? You'll also find advisors with good credentials who simply aren't attentive to your specific needs. You explain your situation and although they hear what you have to say, they still go off in another direction. Perhaps this is the only manner in which the advisor has been trained to proceed with every client that comes through the door. It's as if your words were never really heard. Remember, **good listening skills are an absolute necessity for a financial advisor.** In conclusion, your relationship with your financial advisor should be an ongoing one in which you have, above all, trust and mutual respect. If even one of those is missing, the relationship is doomed to fail. And if that's the case, you might as well end the relationship sooner rather than later. You are not doing him a favor by remaining his client. Life is too short, so pull the plug and find a replacement.

Exhibit 10-1

What Does A Financial Advisor Do?

Personal Financial Planning

1. Establishes your goals, objectives, and risk tolerance

2. Collects relevant data regarding your financial situation

3. Assesses your current financial situation

4. Establishes reasonable assumptions for use in the planning process (e.g., inflation, rate of return, longevity)

5. Prepares a financial plan to meet your financial goals

6. Implements or assists you in implementing your financial plan

7. Monitors your financial situation and updates your financial plan as necessary

Income Tax Planning

8. Advises you regarding the federal and state income tax consequences of financial decisions (keeps you out of "trouble" with the IRS)

9. Helps you minimize tax liabilities through the use of various techniques

10. Advises you on the issues related to your personal decisions, such as life events (e.g., marriage, divorce, birth of a family member, etc.)

Risk Management Planning

11. Analyzes your exposure to risk and reviews methods for managing that risk

12. Advises you on various types of insurance and their uses

13. Helps you minimize your financial risks (e.g., from disability, illness, long-term care, property damage, and personal and professional liability)

14. Reviews current insurance policies to ensure your needs are satisfied

15. Reviews with you the income, estate, and investment aspects of your insurance coverage

Investment Planning

16. Reviews with you your investment preferences and risk tolerance, and help you develop an appropriate rate-of-return strategy to meet your financial goals

17. Develops asset allocation recommendations

18. Discusses available options, and associated risk with those options, with you. This may include the utilization of *Monte Carlo Simulation* to determine the probability of achieving the objectives with each option.

19. Recommends appropriate investments and helps you build a portfolio

20. Implements the selected investment strategies

Investment Planning (cont'd)

21. Monitors the performance of invested assets

22. Plans for capital gains and losses (e.g., loss recognition planning and deferral of capital gains, harvesting long-term capital gains for charitable contributions)

23. Rebalances portfolio periodically as agreed upon

Retirement Planning

24. Helps you develop and quantify your retirement planning goals

25. Develops retirement needs analysis that calculates the investment rate of return required to meet your retirement goals and objectives

26. Reviews with you the limits on, and tax consequences of, contributions to, or distributions from your retirement plans

27. Develops a retirement distribution strategy

28. Assists you in determining when to begin your Social Security benefits

Estate and Gift Planning

29. Helps you develop or refine your estate planning goals

30. Estimates liabilities for federal estate tax, state death taxes and other obligations, and determines liquidity requirements at death

31. Develops recommendations to meet financial obligations and administrative responsibilities associated with death

32. Reviews with you the tax and probate considerations of various forms of property ownership, and makes recommendations on the titling of assets

33. Develops strategies for transferring assets (e.g., estate and death taxes), and achieving your other estate planning goals

34. Recommends or reviews various instruments (wills, powers of attorney, trusts, etc.) for use in achieving estate planning goals

35. Develops a plan or strategies for charitable giving and/or lifetime gifting, if needed

Education Planning

36. Reviews and quantifies educational cash requirements

37. Determines the appropriate vehicles for setting aside funds for education

38. Helps you determine financial aid eligibility

39. Develops and implements a plan to fund educational cash requirements

In Summary

40. Helps the client make smart financial decisions to help him/her get to, and stay, *On Golden Pond*.

Chapter 11

Conclusion

OKAY, SO THERE you have it—everything you ever wanted to know about planning your own secure retirement but didn't think to ask. I know the task can be daunting at first, but the secret is to not let it overwhelm you. Break the project down into smaller steps with reasonable deadlines for each step. In other words, **create a plan for the plan.**

It is extremely crucial that you begin right away to work on your plan to reach Golden Pond. If you get stuck and your budget can allow for it, do seek the help of a professional, if for no other reason than to get an objective second opinion. If your budget is tight, there are excellent resources in your local library and on the Internet. These resources are available to everybody. If you do not own a computer, you can always use one at the library. If you are serious about your retirement security, you will not let anyone or anything get in your way—certainly not lack of a computer. Remember the adage, "If it's got to be, it's up to me!"

Above all, do not get disheartened and give up on the project. If **Good Luck. I hope to see you soon ON GOLDEN POND!**

About the Author

F. BILL BILLIMORIA has been in the financial advisory business since 1982. Before becoming a financial advisor, he was employed as a management consultant for almost ten years. During his stint as a consultant, Bill traveled extensively. He was often out of town on business from Sunday afternoon to Friday evening for weeks at a time. As a result, he did not have much time to devote to the family finances, and on several occasions, he trusted the wrong "advisor." He made every mistake in the book and lost a lot of precious money and even more precious time. In this way, he received his financial education through the school of hard knocks. When he realized that he was in danger of being laid off due to an economic slow-down, Bill decided to venture into the very field where he had been victimized. He resolved to help people who did not have the time or expertise to handle their own finances.

In the early stages of his new career, Bill had hardly any clients to speak of, and he often felt like a Maytag repairman. Nevertheless, he persevered in this demanding profession to the point where he is now regarded as one of the top advisors in the country.

In addition to his experience as a management consultant and a financial advisor, Bill has a vast educational background. He has undergraduate and graduate degrees in industrial engineering from the Illinois Institute of Technology in Chicago and an MBA in finance from the University of Chicago. Additionally, he is certified in public accounting (CPA), management accounting (CMA), and financial planning (CFP). He has also received the Personal Finance Specialist (PFS) designation from the American Institute of Certified Public Accountants.

Bill has appeared as a guest on several radio stations across the country for his views on matters related to investments, income taxes, and personal finance. He has conducted numerous seminars and workshops for businesses, organizations, and the general public. He describes his talks as "edutainment" because he entertains the audience through humor while imparting a serious message at the same time.